AN ELIZABETHAN PROGRESS

A rare representation of Elizabeth I on horseback (from the Great Seal of England, 1584–6, reverse).

AN ELIZABETHAN PROGRESS

The Queen's Journey into East Anglia, 1578

Zillah Dovey

SUTTON PUBLISHING

First published in the United Kingdom in 1996 by
Alan Sutton Publishing Ltd, an imprint of Sutton Publishing Limited
Phoenix Mill · Thrupp · Stroud · Gloucestershire GL5 2BU

Paperback edition first published in 1999 by Sutton Publishing Limited

British Library Cataloguing in Publication Data

A catalogue record for this book is available from the British Library.

ISBN 0-7509-2150-1

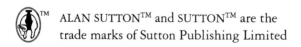 ALAN SUTTON™ and SUTTON™ are the
trade marks of Sutton Publishing Limited

Typeset in 11/13 Garamond.
Typesetting and origination by
Sutton Publishing Limited.
Printed in Great Britain by
Butler and Tanner, Frome, Somerset.

To Hugh
with love and thanks for everything

Set me fine Spanish tables in the hall;
See they be fitted all;
Let there be room to eat
And order taken that there want no meat.
See every sconce and candlestick made bright,
That without tapers they may give a light.
Look to the presence; are the carpets spread,
The dazie o'er the head,
The cushions in the chairs,
And all the candles lighted on the stairs?
Perfume the chambers, and in any case
Let each man give attendance in his place!

Anon: *The New Oxford Book of English Verse*

CONTENTS

LIST OF ILLUSTRATIONS

FOREWORD

by David Loades

Elizabethan England was a highly personal monarchy. All renaissance monarchies were shaped by the personalities of their rulers, but England was a particularly outstanding example. Unlike her highly conventional half-sister Mary, Elizabeth realized that her sex could be a weapon, to baffle and disarm the men with whom she constantly had to deal, both at home and abroad. A casual glance would suggest that half of Europe was being ruled by women in the 1560s – the 'monstrous regiment' so much deplored by John Knox – but the appearance would be deceptive. Catherine de Medici was Regent for her young son Charles IX, but it is doubtful whether she was ever really in control of France. Margaret of Parma was Regent of the Netherlands, but Philip II gave her so little authority that her task became impossible. Mary Stuart was Queen of Scotland in her own right, but in less than a decade the storms generated by her own passionate indiscretions had swept her away. Only Elizabeth endured, and was undisputably mistress of her realm.

By 1578 she was forty-five, and had been on the throne for twenty years. Moreover she was unmarried, an eccentric condition which solved one set of problems, but only at the cost of producing another. Freed from the present fear of an unsuitable king, foreign or domestic, politically minded Englishmen looked beyond the Queen's life with apprehension. After the death of Catherine Grey, Countess of Hertford, in 1568, the obvious heir was the deplorable Mary Stuart; not only a foreigner but a Catholic. Once the pope had declared war on Elizabeth in the bull *Regnans in excelsis* of 1570, England's integrity as a sovereign state became inseparable from its Protestantism. Where was a good Protestant successor to be found? It required great faith to place much trust in the young King of Scots, tossed by the conflicting factions of that unstable kingdom.

Nevertheless, circumstances had conspired in Elizabeth's favour. The collapse of Mary's position in Scotland, and the continuing civil war in France meant that England was free from the shadow of the Auld Alliance, which had loomed so large in Henry VIII's time. The Anglo-French treaty of 1572 may not have contributed much to England's security, but it was a symbol of a new diplomatic orientation. By contrast, relations with Spain were deteriorating year by year, and Philip's crusading instincts threatened a counter-reformation with a military as well as an evangelical face. Fortunately, in 1576 the King of Spain had become bankrupt, and his unpaid armies had sacked the city of Antwerp, turning the small scale revolt in Holland and Zeeland into a major conflagration. In 1578 Philip had his hands full in the Low Countries, and had neither time nor money to spare for a side swipe at the heretical and provocative English. Elizabeth could hardly afford tranquillity. Roberto Ridolphi had failed to have her assassinated, but others would try, and it was impossible not to regard recusant gentlemen as a potential fifth column, however much they might resent the aspersions cast on their loyalty. At the same time, for reasons best known to herself, the queen was about to pick up again the scent of the Anjou marriage, which had seemed to go cold several years before. Whether her motives were diplomatic or personal has never been determined, and probably never will, but when she set out on her summer progress in 1578 her councillors were already eyeing the evidence for this latest eccentricity with doubt and concern. Consequently they had much to exercise their minds as they ambled through the East Anglian countryside, hoping that the harbingers and couriers were up to the task of keeping them comfortable and in touch while their mistress soaked up the adulation so carefully displayed for her benefit.

Adulation was neither a luxury nor a self-indulgence as far as Elizabeth was concerned. The loyalty of her subjects constituted the backbone of the state. With neither a standing army nor a professional police force, the coercive resources of the Crown were extremely limited. Moreover, suppressing rebellions, even quite small ones such as that which had afflicted the far north of England in 1569, cost a great deal of money. Obedience, based upon a willing devotion, was not only cheaper, it was very much more effective. Elizabeth knew perfectly well that loyalty depended partly upon what she did, and partly upon what she was. Thomas Norton struck the required note when he informed the House of Commons in 1571

'. . . our sovereigne Ladye . . . is the most noble natured prince in the worlde, and therewith both so wise as she would not have so farre trusted you yf she had not bene resolved well to [do] and so gratious as she will well allowe of all trewe and plaine and honeste meaninge . . .'

Coming from a man of Norton's strong convictions, such support was not unconditional, and Elizabeth understood, without ever openly admitting, that her freedom of action was constrained by the need to carry the political nation with her. In that she could be greatly assisted by projecting the right image, and by a judicious display of graciousness and affability. In spite of her imperious nature, the Queen knew that she had to be a persuader, and in the summer of 1578 she probably realized that her skill in that direction would be tested to the limit when it became known that she seriously intended to marry the Duke of Anjou. At the same time the symbolism of the reign was beginning to gain momentum and coherence. The first recorded Accession Day tournament had been held in November 1577, and Richard

Day's *Booke of Christian Prayers*, published in 1578, placed the Queen in that position of honour traditionally occupied by the Blessed Virgin in the *Horae* of the old faith. The summer progress of 1578 was not a unique, or even an exceptional event, but it does provide a very good example of Elizabeth's political style. There was no great crisis to curtail it, or distract from its impact, and the Queen enjoyed herself because it gave her exactly what she wanted.

There were good reasons for going to Norfolk. Norwich, with about 16,000 inhabitants, was the second city of the kingdom, although less than a tenth of the size of London, and the county was populous and prosperous. Twenty-five years earlier East Anglia had provided the core of Mary's political support, and loyalty to the Howards was still evident. The Duke of Norfolk's arrest and execution had taken place only six years before. Norfolk was also a county in which both recusants and puritans were numerous. Without the coherent political leadership that the Howards had provided, substantial gentry families, such as the Bacons, the Gawdys and the Heydons, jostled for patronage and prestige. Several of these families had strong Court connections, and stood to gain from a royal visit to their home area. Although some distance from the capital, Norwich was not remote, and Norfolk was overdue for some attention. Perhaps Elizabeth had been deterred by the spectre of the Robsarts of Syderstone, since Amy's dramatic death in 1560 had ended any hopes which she might have entertained of marrying Robert Dudley. Her old gaoler, Sir Henry Bedingfield of Oxborough, was still very much alive, his own and his family's determined adherence to the old faith making them doubly inimical. However, if the Queen had any aversion to Norfolk or its inhabitants, it was not allowed to appear. The number and importance of the recusant gentlemen cast a shadow across her path, but they were a problem for the Council, not for Elizabeth herself. She did not mind whose hospitality was constrained on her behalf, as long as a decent show of enthusiasm was sustained.

We also know a good deal more about the Norfolk progress than we do about most other such events because two eye-witness accounts were recorded and survive: Bernard Garter's 'The Ioyfull Receyving of the Queenes most excellent Maiestie into hir Highnesse Citie of Norwich', and Thomas Churchyard's 'A Discourse of the Queenes Maiesties entertainement in Suffolk and Norfolk'. Churchyard was one of the principal devisers of the entertainments in Norwich, having been seconded from the Court for that purpose, and neither of the accounts could be described as objective, but that is of no great significance. Both are full of circumstantial details which could not be recovered in any other way. This information is not unknown to scholars. John Nichols used it a hundred and fifty years ago in *The Progresses and Public Processions of Queen Elizabeth*, a work which is now rare, and known only to specialists. More recently Ian Dunlop presented a brief account of the same events in *Palaces and Progresses of Elizabeth I* (1962), but what Zillah Dovey has done in the following pages is to reconstruct the whole progress in full from beginning to end, with many fascinating insights into the organization of the Court during such an adventure. It is very seldom that we can come so close to the people and their preoccupations, to ride with them day by day, and share their satisfaction in a job well done. The Norfolk progress of 1578 opens a unique window on the sixteenth century.

David Loades
University College of North Wales, Bangor

ACKNOWLEDGEMENTS

My thanks are due to the staff of the libraries, record offices and picture libraries, and to other owners of source material, who have all been unfailingly helpful. Among others to whom I am grateful are Dr Philip Tennant, who introduced me to Alan Sutton Publishing; Dr Alan Crosby, whose lectures and book on the history of Thetford reinforced my interest in this progress; Marion Colthorpe MA, who pointed to several invaluable sources; Guy Avery, who patiently produced alternative versions of his drawings; Bobby, Lady Hooper, who housed me during my researches in London; Estelle Clark, who gave me much-needed time to work on the book; and, most of all, my husband, Hugh, for moral support and practical assistance.

Many of the illustrations are reproduced by the kind permission of the following copyright holders: The National Trust (pp. 8, 42, 92); The British Library (pp. 9, 53, 58); The Museum of London (pp. 11, 152); The Syndics of Cambridge University Library (pp. 35); The Controller HM Stationery Office (p. 24); The Royal Collection © 1995 Her Majesty the Queen (p. 32); English Heritage, Audley End House (p. 32) Kedington PCC (p. 41); Staatliche Museen Kassel (p. 44); The National Portrait Gallery, London (pp. 46, 82, 150, 151); The Marquess of Salisbury (pp. 56, 90); His Grace the Duke of Norfolk (p. 60); Norwich Castle Museum, Norfolk Museums Service (pp. 64, 73); Norfolk County Council Library and Information Service (p. 67); The Burrell Collection, Glasgow Museums (p. 96); The Tate Gallery, London (p. 105); The Cambridgeshire Collection, Cambridgeshire Libraries (p. 115); The Bodleian Library, Oxford (p. 116); Essex Record Office (p. 126); Hertfordshire Record Office (p. 131); Sotheby's, London (p. 139); Northamptonshire Record Society (p. 143); The Public Record Office (pp. ii, 19, 145); The Marquess of Bath, Longleat House, Warminster, Wilts (p. 150); Courtauld Institute of Art (pp. 8, 60, 119, 135); Guy Avery (pp. 13, 37, 51, 70); John McCann (p. 28); Studio 5, Thetford (pp. 41, 71, 100, 111, 113); Sir Richard Hyde Parker (p. 42); Hatfield House (p. 56).

INTRODUCTION

The Queen enjoyed her summer expeditions. She and her Court were used to moving up and down the Thames – they shifted regularly between the palaces of Greenwich, Whitehall, Richmond, Hampton Court, Oatlands and Windsor – and the mechanics of removal were matters of routine. Furnishings, hangings and so on were regularly taken down, brushed and aired and put up somewhere else; then the rooms vacated could be cleaned. But in the summer the Queen like to get away from London and show herself to her people. Progresses were primarily an exercise in image-making. To establish and maintain her personal popularity among her people was one of the Queen's major – and successful – policies. As the Spanish ambassador reported in 1568, 'She was received everywhere with great acclamations and signs of joy as is customary in this country whereat she was exceedingly pleased.'[1] Wherever she went the church bells were rung and crowds gathered. To the ordinary people, though not always to her Council and courtiers, she was accessible and patient. She could, said Thomas Churchyard, always an admirer, 'draw the hearts of the people after hyr wheresoever she travels'.

So Elizabeth made a summer progress whenever she could, which meant in almost every year until the end of the 1570s. She travelled less often and less far as she got older and times more dangerous, but she went off again in the last four years of her life. In 1600, when she was sixty-seven and her ministers tried to dissuade her from moving on from the palace of Nonsuch, she retorted that the old could stay behind if they wished, the young and able would go with her;[2] and in what was to be her last summer, two years later, it was reported that 'notwithstanding her earnest affection to go her Progress', out of compassion for her entourage, she had agreed to take heed of the unseasonable weather.[3]

In the course of her long reign she covered a good deal of southern England, sometimes staying within the Home Counties but often travelling as far as Southampton, Bristol, Worcester, Warwick and Stafford. Such journeys served not only to give many people a once-in-a-lifetime chance to catch a glimpse of their sovereign but also to show the Queen herself something of the more distant parts of her realm. However, that said, she never went to the south-west or further north than Stafford – or out of England.

With her had to go her Court, the environment in which she lived and worked wherever she was. The basic necessities of her life, and of course of all those who went

1

with her, were the responsibility of the Lord Steward, the chief officer of the Household. He was in charge of the expenditure through the Treasurer of the Household, the Controller and the Cofferer (who made up the 'Board of Greencloth') and their Clerks of the Counting House, all of whom travelled with the Queen. The services needed to maintain the Court were provided by twenty Household departments, each with its particular job – the bakehouse, the larder, the spicery, the kitchen, the cellar, the buttery, the laundry and so on. When the Court moved, all of these went too. The other, external, side of the Queen's life, her handsome lifestyle, was headed by the Lord Chamberlain. With the Vice-Chamberlain and the Treasurer of the Chamber, he was responsible for the Chamber. His staff of ushers, grooms and pages looked after her accommodation, her wardrobe (with her ladies and her maids), her entertainments and her travels. Her guards, her chaplains and the court musicians were also Chamber personnel. All these too had work to do wherever the Queen might be.

Also during a progress affairs of state had to continue as usual; it was by no means a holiday. The Queen with her Council constituted the government of the country and where she was they had to be. The Council consisted of between seventeen and twenty chief officers of state and of the Court, and a varying but limited number of these moved between palaces or across the country with her. Their business had to be conducted on the wing, their meetings held as necessary wherever they and she happened to be. The Queen was rarely present; on all subjects of sufficient importance her views would be sought and reported by one or other of the councillors. Their decisions were recorded and submitted for her approval. Then instructions would be sent to ambassadors abroad or to local authorities at home, sheriffs of counties, Justices of the Peace or others who had commissions to carry out particular assignments. The Council met frequently and a steady stream of visitors, messengers and couriers flowed to and fro, however temporary their bases. It is remarkable how rarely letters from Council members mentioned their travels; usually the only indication is the superscription 'from the Court at' such and such a place or, often, 'from the house of' so and so. Everyone involved was accustomed to this peripatetic way of conducting affairs.

Nevertheless, for her ministers and officials and their servants, progresses must have been uncomfortable and inconvenient. They involved a considerable effort in organization and administration, even if the procedures were more or less established routine. A great many arrangements had to be made in advance, but plans also had to be flexible and were often altered because of the Queen's inclinations, the weather or, most importantly, the plague. When finally they set off, for most of the several hundred people who accompanied the Queen, the great Court and state officials, all with their own staff, working and living conditions were considerably less satisfactory than in their quarters in and around the royal palaces.

Travelling was difficult and slow even on the main highways and cross-country roads were little more than tracks made by use. In 1555 the maintenance of the roads had become the responsibility of each parish, but they were required to work on them only four, later six, days a year. At best they cut down the undergrowth and filled in the pot-holes with stones, and the results were patchy and unreliable. Complaints about poor conditions continued to the end of the century. Even in 1607 there was no attempt at drainage. There were few hedges or fences, so roads could change course to avoid obstacles.

A man on horseback was the fastest form of travel, changing horses at intervals on the way (royal couriers had warrants to commandeer horses). Even so, on a long journey he would cover little more than 4 miles an hour. Goods went by packhorse or wagon. Coaches had come into use in the mid-sixteenth century but, though the Queen did sometimes use one on progress, they were uncomfortable on good and impossible on the many bad roads. Similarly a litter carried by men or horses was suitable only for the town or city.

Mostly, the Queen and her retinue rode, but they were preceded or accompanied by an immense baggage train, between 200 and 300 two- or four-wheeled carts drawn by teams of six horses, carrying everything necessary for the Queen, the Court and the Council – bedding, furniture, hangings, clothing, plate and kitchen equipment, documents and office requirements. The main body moved 10 to 12 miles a day.

The Queen went from house to house, in the Home Counties sometimes staying in a palace of her own but more often in the houses of her subjects, from national figures to local gentlemen. Her usual practice was to arrive before supper, towards the end of the afternoon or in the early evening, and to leave after dinner in the late morning. Alternatively, on a longer stage, the start might be earlier and she would stop for dinner at another house – or perhaps, if none was suitable, a picnic – on the way. The ministers and courtiers who travelled with her were lodged in other houses in the neighbourhood. Inevitably, there were disputes over their accommodation, which could not always be appropriate for the status of everyone. The rest of the officials and their servants put up wherever they could, in inns or even in the tents which were always carried to provide stabling for the horses and housing for their keepers. When stationary, the whole train was scattered over a considerable distance.

Naturally, the Queen gave the final word, but the planning of a progress was left to the Privy Council, which included the major officers of the Court. Two of these, the Lord Chamberlain and the Vice-Chamberlain, were responsible for the detailed preparation and the day-to-day management.

Early in the year likely houses where the Queen might stay along the route were inspected by Court officers, who reported on their suitability or otherwise, looking particularly at the outlook and surroundings and whether there was plague in the area. The Queen's lodging places were selected for their comfort and convenience (the houses where she stopped for dinner were not inspected in the same way). According to feudal tradition, the sovereign, from whom in principle all manors were ultimately held, retained the right to occupy any subject's house, so the Chamber officers simply took over wherever it was thought best for the Queen to stay; the owners, if they were not rich or important figures, were disregarded.

Later, other officers, the harbingers, went ahead looking for lodgings for the Court and Council and their staff.

Finally, the Queen's 'gestes', itineraries in the form of lists of lodgings, were published at Court (without precise dates) and copies sent to mayors of towns and Lord-Lieutenants of counties, who had to confirm that there was no plague in their areas. Towns and villages were ordered to provide stocks of food, fuel and fodder, which would then be bought up by the Purveyors, who organized all the regular supplies for the Royal Household. A Yeoman Purveyor and his deputy were assigned to an area with a Royal Commission 'to take up and provide for us and our name for the only provision of our household in all places'.[4] The commission went on to refer to 'our reasonable prices', which were fixed by the Queen's Clerk of the Market, who also checked the local weights and measures to see that the Purveyors were not cheated. The system was unpopular and the Purveyors were frequently accused of corruption; areas which were regularly visited by the Queen could be exempted. Similarly, although the Queen's stables never held less than 220 horses, transport could, when needed, be commandeered by the Yeoman Cart-taker and his three grooms, who were supposed to pay 2d a mile.

Nearer the time, prospective hosts were told the approximate date of the Queen's arrival. What they were expected to provide varied according to their circumstances; for minor country gentlemen of modest means, it would be only a clean, empty house, the family having moved out at least from the main rooms. Supplies would be provided through the purveyance system or paid for by the Counting House, though no doubt the machinery of reimbursement moved slowly. The Queen herself was unwilling to cause her subjects too much expense, though naturally more was expected of the wealthy and ambitious, who were anxious to display their loyalty.

A few days before the Queen was due to arrive, a team of eight to ten men would come to make arrangements for the Queen's accommodation. They were led by a Gentleman Usher, whose regular job was the management of the Queen's public rooms and control of all who entered and left. A little later an officer of the Wardrobe of Robes with a smaller team would come 'to make reddye the office of Her Majesty's roabes'. They all came, whether the Queen was staying several days or stopping for dinner, the length of their stay varying according to the expected length of hers. If she was to stay for her usual two nights, the ushers normally took six days and the Robes men three. If she was coming only for dinner, the ushers would stay two days and the Robes one. On progress the ushers created appropriately furnished rooms to match those in her palaces: an audience or presence chamber which was open to anyone with a right to be at Court (everyone, however important, had to have permission both to come to Court and to leave) and was where entertainments were held; a privy chamber, where the less public business took place; and a withdrawing chamber or bedchamber, which was private to all but the Queen's ladies and a few favoured courtiers. Each room or suite of rooms led into the next and the doors between them were guarded.

A good deal of careful planning had to be done before the ushers set off. Each had to arrive at a house in good time to get all ready, stay until the Queen left, then take down and pack up everything his team had brought and move on. There had therefore to be several teams on the road. While the Queen was at one house, attended by one team, another would have gone ahead to prepare the next stopping place. Often a single team worked on two houses, one where she would be staying and another about half-way to the next, where she would have dinner on the day she left. They would then move on to another house, which the Queen was due to reach some days later. The Wardrobe officers followed a similar, though less regular, leapfrogging pattern.

At least in the main stopping places, there also had to be a room where the Council could meet and an adjoining one for their clerks, who brought the 'paper pennes inke waxe and other necessaries' for their work. In the royal palaces and perhaps in some other great houses, the Keeper of the Counsell Chamber also saw that it was embellished with 'bowes' (branches) and flowers.

There might also be a visit by the Controller of Works, who was responsible for the maintenance of the royal palaces and would carry out work on other people's houses as well, such as improving the door locks, if necessary.

Other officers from the Jewel House at the Tower of London brought silver plate for use at the Queen's table and to ornament the rooms she would use. Finally, the Court officers had to be supplied with money to meet their running costs and some of their clerks would bring the coin from the City of London. In spite of all the hospitality received on its travels, the Court on progress added £2,000 a year to its usual budget. Changes of plan en route added particularly to the cost, requiring supplies and staff to be redirected and relocated.

In areas where a regular royal mail service was not normally in place, special arrangements had to be made for the Council and Court to receive and dispatch their reports and instructions. Post horses were stationed every 10 miles or so along a route and were ridden from one post to the next by the courier, the horses being returned to their bases by a postboy. On routes with permanent, as distinct from ad hoc, arrangements, the letters would be carried from post to post by a rider stationed at each point who would hand over the packet to the next man and return to his own base.

All these people arriving with their horses – at least two each – had to be fed and housed while they carried out the Queen's business.

The owners of the great houses where the Queen stayed two or three days gave lavish feasts and entertainments, sometimes going to enormous lengths to provide spectacular 'shows' – and there was always a personal present for the Queen, as well as gifts for courtiers and officials. The costs were enormous and a visit could make or break a man's political career. No wonder the prospect was likely to cause anxiety, particularly among the less eminent gentlemen, even if the Queen was coming only for dinner in the middle of the day or staying for one night.

For the towns where the Queen stayed, a visit brought honour and opportunity but also demanded expenditure of both effort and money. There were formal occasions with loyal greetings by the mayor and corporation or the guilds, feasts and entertainments. The streets were cleaned, buildings were painted, new civic gowns were made. Shows and pageants were arranged; on some occasions, they were master-minded by professionals sent on ahead by the Lord Chamberlain. The Queen was always presented with a gift, frequently including cash in gold. In all it was an expensive occasion.

The incidental costs could be high too, with an invasion by a large number of officials, servants and hangers-on looking for gifts, bribes, and board and lodging. Property could be damaged and objects disappear. An even greater burden might be brought by the invaders from London in the shape of the plague. London had by far the largest, most densely housed population in the country and outbreaks of plague there were common. They caused the law courts to be adjourned thirty-five times during Elizabeth's reign. The Court made every effort to safeguard the Queen's health, but they could not protect everyone who came into contact with their vast and varied train.

CHAPTER 1

TWO PROGRESSES
1 MAY–11 JULY

A Minor Progress

At eight o'clock on May Day morning the Queen was standing in a gallery in Greenwich Palace, looking out over the tiltyard. She was not yet dressed in the finery in which she appeared in public – all the pinning and tying by her maids took a long time – and was still in her nightclothes. Walking below was Gilbert Talbot, the 25-year-old son of the Earl of Shrewsbury. He looked up and saw the Queen full in view, clearly in a state of undress. Elizabeth showed herself disconcerted – as well she might, for Gilbert was a great gossip. Fortunately for him, she was in a good temper that day. When after her late morning dinner taken in private, she appeared, suitably dressed, in the presence chamber, she encountered Gilbert again. As she passed she gave him 'a great phylypp', a sharp tap, on his forehead with a fan or such and told the Lord Chamberlain who was walking with her how she had been embarrassed that morning.[1]

It was not always so. The Queen's temper was notoriously uncertain and in 1578 pains in her face often made her difficult to deal with. In April her physicians had concluded that her toothache could be cured only by an extraction, but they dared not tell her so. Lord Treasurer Burghley, her chief minister, suggested that Sir Christopher Hatton, her Vice-Chamberlain, should do it. Only 'some one tooth' needed to be 'withdrawn', he said, but, 'Except that be removed Her Majesty's pain shall not be quit.'[2] Hatton was devoted to the Queen – he never married – and was a favourite among her courtiers, but even he seems not to have had the temerity to give her the doctors' advice, for she continued to suffer intermittently during the summer.

At the end of the financial year, in September 1578, the wages of her two apothecaries were recorded, £11 2s 6d each for the year. Payments for 'apothecarye stuffe' provided 'for Her Majesty's owne person and employed for and in hir highenes paynes at sundrie tymes' totalled over £289, an enormous amount compared with

Greenwich Palace from the River Thames, first half of the seventeenth century.

their wages. The highest expenditure had been in the winter quarter, October–December 1577, but it was lowest in the spring, when the Queen took a short break from her usual duties. As predicted earlier by the inquisitive Gilbert Talbot, for ten days in May she was away, making a 'little Progress' along the valley of the River Lea in Essex. This was a real holiday, with less formality than normally characterized her life in the royal palaces and on her major progresses. Nor was there as much business of state to attend to; from 6 to 16 May there were no Privy Council meetings, though several members went with her, and there was 'no Chamber kept' (that is, there was no presence chamber where she would give public audiences). All but the first of the five houses she stayed in had a deer park, so she was able indulge in one of her favourite pastimes, hunting.

All the essential preparations had to be made before her arrival at each house; comfortable and appropriate rooms had to be ready. For this informal trip, only a suite of outer and inner rooms to use as privy chamber and bedchamber would be needed. But the Queen would still expect a stock of suitable clothes and ornaments to be available, so Raphe Hope, Yeoman of Her Majesty's Wardrobe of Robes, went ahead, accompanied by at least one personal servant. He would have arrived before her

Hunting – the Queen is offered a knife to make the first cut (Turbervile's *Booke of Hunting*, 1576).

at each of the five houses and left again to be ready at the next house in time. At Theobalds, where she stayed longest, he remained in attendance for the whole of her visit. For at least some of the time he was helped in the scheduling of his moves by the presence of Charles Smythe, Page of Her Majesty's Wardrobe of Robes, a less important but not necessarily younger officer. He was away eleven days in all, a day longer than the Queen.

Similarly three Officers of the Removing (that is, mobile) Wardrobe of Beds, which was responsible for all the furniture required by the Queen outside her London palaces, went, each with his own servants, to the five houses. Working a schedule of leapfrogging visits, they carried, or appropriated locally, everything that might be needed to organize and equip the Queen's rooms. First an officer with a groom – his subordinate official – and two labourers went to Tottenham and on from there to Copthall. The second similar team took another set of furnishings to Theobalds. They stayed while the Queen was there and then packed up and went on to Wanstead, again staying to take down and pack up everything after she had gone. Meanwhile, the third team, an officer, a groom and four labourers, set up the royal suite at Stanstead Abbots, attended the Queen during her stay there and then dismantled everything and sent it on to Copthall, where the first group was already waiting. When it arrived they had to get ready for the Queen's coming that same day. They too remained during her stay and then, when she had gone, took down and dismantled everything, sending it all back to store in London.

Work had also been carried out at all five houses by Thomas Fowler, newly appointed Gentleman Controller of All and Every Her Highness Works. On this occasion he was concerned mainly with the security of the Queen's rooms. Some locks were portable. When the Queen stayed outside her own houses, they could be brought and fitted to the doors of the rooms she would occupy. The keys would be handed to whichever appropriate Court official was there. At Tottenham Fowler's work cost as much as $19s\ 8d$ and a Wanstead $17s\ 4d$. Less had had to be done at the others: $14s\ 2d$ at Copthall, $12s\ 6d$ at Theobalds and only $10s\ 4d$ at Stanstead Abbots.[3]

Elizabeth set out from Greenwich on Tuesday 6 May.[4] She was accompanied by some of her councillors and officers of her Household. Others, as indicated above, were already in place at the houses she was to visit. She was attended by four Ordinary (regularly employed) Gentleman Ushers, important Chamber officers who would be in charge of the rooms she would use, controlling all who entered and left. Among the four were Anthony Wingfeld, who rode ahead with his two men to each house to see that all was ready, and Symon Bowyer (both appear again later). They were paid $2s$ per day. They had a staff of eight Gentlemen Waiters and Shewers (servers) – gentlemen assistants to the Ushers – who were paid $1s\ 8d$ per day, and ten Ordinary Grooms at $1s$ per day each. Among these was Richard Lecavell, who had been sent away from Court for twelve days on full pay the previous October because

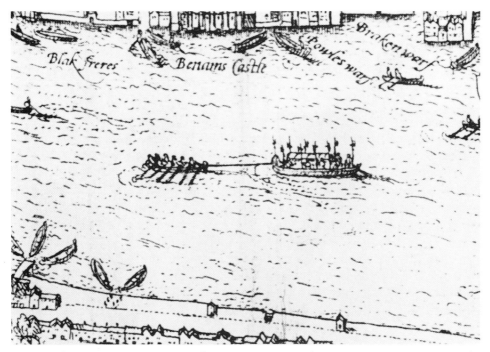

The royal barge on the Thames (detail from Braun and Hogenberg map, 1575). There seem to be Gentlemen Pensioners with their distinctive halberds stationed round the barge outside the canopy.

someone had died of the plague on his premises. There was also a Francis Fearrett, who attended the Queen for the ten days 'by hir highenes commandment' with his man and their horses.

On that Tuesday Elizabeth travelled about 10 miles, a journey which began by barge across the Thames and probably some way up the River Lea. Her first stop was at Lord Compton's house at Tottenham, where she stayed one night. Henry VIII had granted three Tottenham manors to Sir William Compton, who died in 1528, a rich man. The house he built there was visited by Henry himself in 1516. It was inherited by his grandson, Sir Henry, later Lord Compton, and now, sixty years later, Elizabeth followed in her father's footsteps. (She had already visited Lord Compton at his other house, Compton Wynyates, in Warwickshire six years earlier.) As soon as the royal party arrived, 'a litell fanne of flowers' was found to be missing and Raphe Hope was sent back to Westminster for it.

Her move on the following day involved a rather shorter journey, to Lord Burghley's house, Theobalds, near Cheshunt. Burghley had been in the Queen's service since her accession in 1558. He became Lord Treasurer of England in 1572 and was to hold that high office until his death in 1598. He had begun to build this house in 1564, continually embellishing and extending it. (In the next century his son Robert was to exchange it with James I for Hatfield House.) Elizabeth obviously liked the house and had already visited it five times; she was to come again on several further occasions, each visit involving her host in a great deal of expenditure. According to Gilbert Talbot, she was expected to stay three or four days, and the Court was certainly there until Saturday 10 May. This time it was Charles Smythe who rode back to fetch a Cloth of Estate from Windsor. Evidently some formal occasions were now expected when it would be hung above the Queen's chair as a symbol of her regal status.

On the Saturday, still travelling north, the Queen moved 8 miles or so to Stanstead Abbots, another house she already knew, having stayed there in 1571 and 1576. This was the house of Edward Baesh, son-in-law of Sir Raphe Sadler, who was to entertain her later in the year. The manor had formerly belonged to the Abbey of Waltham Cross, but he had acquired it some time after the Dissolution of the Monasteries.[5] Baesh was, as recorded on his monument in Stanstead church, 'General Surveyor of Victuals for the Navy Royal and Marine Affairs within the Realms of England and Ireland', a post he had managed to hold under Mary Tudor, Edward VI and Elizabeth. He was also an MP first for Rochester and later, with Sadler's influence, for Preston. When the Queen came he was seventy-one, and he was to die, a poor man despite the opportunities offered by his position, at the age of eighty. Elizabeth stayed in his house two nights.

Some time earlier, Secretary of State Sir Francis Walsingham had heard from the English agent in Antwerp of a unicorn's horn being offered for sale to the Queen by someone in the Netherlands. While he was at Stanstead, he had time to deal with this rather minor matter and he wrote discouragingly to Antwerp. The Queen, he said, was not 'so much affected to buying jewels as her father was'. (Gifts were obviously quite a different matter.)

This was the furthest point of her journey and on Monday 12 May Elizabeth turned south-east and crossed the River Lea. Another short stage and she reached Copthall near Epping, which she had first visited in 1568. This was the home of Sir Thomas Heneage, the Treasurer of her Chamber, who was responsible for the Court's expenditure. Originally from Lincolnshire, he too had benefited indirectly from the Dissolution and had built his new house on land formerly owned by Waltham Abbey which he had been granted in 1564. It was remarkable for the length of its long gallery – 56 yards.[6]

Heneage was of course well known to her; he had been appointed to the Privy Chamber in 1560 and had received his knighthood in the December before this visit. Later in life he was to rise even higher in her service, becoming Vice-Chamberlain in 1589 and in 1593, two years before his death, Chancellor of the Duchy of Lancaster.

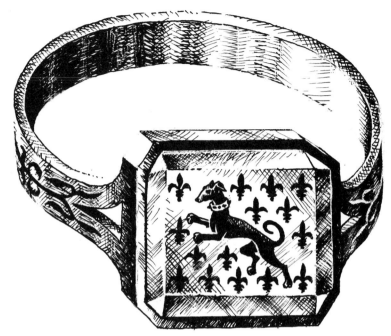

Sir Thomas Heneage's 1579 New Year gift (artist's impression).

He was also an MP, first for Boston and later for Essex, and Recorder of Colchester. Heneage was devoted to the Queen and left her in his will a jewel, saying it was for her 'who above all other earthly Creatures I have thought most wourthie of all my hartes love and reverence'.[7] Elizabeth stayed only one night, but while she was at his house she wore a velvet cloak with a gold jewel which Sir Thomas had given her earlier – Raphe Hope had been sent off especially to bring it to Copthall. The following New Year he was to give her an enamelled gold ring set with a 'white ruby' carved with a greyhound.

The Queen's final stop on her way back to Greenwich was at Wanstead, the house which Lord Leicester had bought only the previous year. A former owner, Lord Rich, had received the Queen there in 1561. This time she arrived on Tuesday 13 May, and Gilbert Talbot expected her to stay four or five days. Robert Dudley, Earl of Leicester, was the closest of the Queen's circle. They were about the same age, now forty-five, and their sometimes stormy personal relationship lasted from before her accession until his death in 1588. Officially he was her Master of the Horse, the third officer of her Household after the Lord Steward and the Lord Chamberlain, responsible for all the Queen's riding horses, packhorses, draught horses and mules, their purchase, breeding and training, their stabling and all the staff involved with them. He was usually in her company.

While she was at Wanstead the entertainments arranged for her included a masque-like play performed in the grounds. Elizabeth enjoyed all theatrical performances, and plays and masques were often put on at Court. This one was special because it was written by Philip Sidney, Leicester's nephew and protégé. He was then aged about twenty-four and was already an established courtier and diplomat. His career as poet and soldier was yet to come; none of his poetic works was published in his lifetime and he was knighted only in 1583, three years before his early death from a bullet wound received at Zutphen in the Netherlands.

The short play, *The Lady of May*, was naturally intended as a flattering tribute to Elizabeth, but it was distinctive in including a parody of the philosophical debates often presented before the Queen by academics. The slight story concerns the lady who asks the Queen to judge between her two suitors, a forester (a gamekeeper who tended his master's deer) and a shepherd. The debate concerns the relative merits of the active and the contemplative life as represented by the two young men and is conducted by rural characters in humorous rustic language. A supporter of the shepherd, for example, says that anyone critical of lamb-like qualities should be 'more odible than a toad in one's porridge'. There is also a schoolmaster whose pompous speech is sprinkled with Latin tags and garbled English. For example, he addresses the Queen thus: 'to you Juno Venus Pallas et profecto plus I have to ostend a mellifluous fruit of my fidelity.' More poetically the two young men end their final songs 'Judge you to whom all beauty's force is lent' and 'Judge you of love to whom all love is bent.' There were also direct references to Lord Leicester: 'a certain gentleman hereby seeks to do you all the honour he can in this house'. At the end the Queen was presented with a simple string of agate beads, an appropriate gift from the rural schoolmaster.8

This was, of course, an early work of the poet whose series of love sonnets *Astrophel and Stella* is vastly better known. Penelope Devereux, who was the real-life Stella, also had links with Wanstead. Later in 1578 her widowed mother was to marry there. In 1581 Penelope herself married Lord Rich, son of the previous owner. Some twenty years later she was to live at Wanstead with her lover Charles Blount, Lord Mountjoy, later Earl of Devonshire, who had recently bought it. In 1605, now divorced, she was to marry him there.9

By now the demands of the state were beginning to make themselves felt. It was from Wanstead on 15 May that the Queen signed a letter to Duke Casimir, son of the Elector Palatine, who was supporting the Protestants in the Netherlands against the Catholic Spanish forces, promising him £20,000. On the same day a more detailed directive to William Davison, the English agent in Antwerp, concerning the dispatch of the money, was signed by a group of councillors, including Lord Burghley and Lord Leicester. The brief holiday was over.

Elizabeth returned to Greenwich the following day and the Council met there on 17 May. In their absence a good deal of spring-cleaning had been done in the palace, as it always was when the Queen was away. The presence chamber, the great chamber, the galleries and the closets had been thoroughly cleaned by the Keeper of Her Majesty's House at Greenwich, who remained in the palace with a skeleton staff when the Court moved out. He paid twelve men 1s per day each to work for four days and nights. And the Keeper of Her Majesty's Standing (permanent) Wardrobe at Greenwich, with his man and four labourers, had spent four days taking down and cleaning the hangings. Finally, Anthony Wingfeld, returning ahead of the Queen, supervised a ten-strong team in 'making readye all the Chambers against Her Ma[jesty']s returne from the litell progresse'. He would have ensured that the Queen's rooms were restored to their expected state.

The next day was Whit Sunday.

Prelude to a Major Progress

The Queen spent the next two months at Greenwich. First there were the Whitsun festivities, for which John Pigion, Yeoman of the Jewel House, had brought a supply of silver plate from the Tower of London, where it was stored when not in use. (During the minor progress Pigion was not employed and the Court would have used the tableware of the rich men with whom the Queen stayed.) Towards the end of May Lord Leicester had permission to leave the Court and travel to Buxton Spa, where he hoped the waters would be good for his bad leg. The Queen missed him and was concerned about his health, particularly, according to Hatton writing to Leicester on 18 June, because he was not accompanied by her physician, Dr Julio Burgurio.[10] As Hatton expected, shortly afterwards she sent 'Dr Julio' to Buxton. He travelled at the Chamber's expense with his two servants and a guide and was back in Greenwich early in July.

In June the Queen's wardrobe was reorganized and extended. Raphe Hope went back and forth along the river from Greenwich to the silkwomen, the mercers and the tailors in the City of London. Their creations replaced a number of gowns and kirtles which had been in store in the Tower and which he took to Greenwich for the Queen to give away. He also took from Greenwich into store her fur-trimmed and fur-lined winter gowns, which would not be needed during the major progress into East Anglia which was now being planned.

Once back in Greenwich, the Privy Council resumed its usual workload, meeting eleven times in May and nineteen more before they left London. They had two major areas of concern. One was the refusal of traditional Catholics to accept the official Protestant religion. They did not believe in the Queen as head of the Church and they could not attend their parish church as required by law; for this the recusants, as they were called, could be fined $12d$ for every Sunday and festival day (£20 per month from 1581). Many were doubtless loyal citizens but particularly after 1570, when Elizabeth was excommunicated by the Pope, Catholicism was regarded as treason and recusants could be pursued with severity.

Religious controversy was inseparable from national politics and fear and suspicion of organized Catholicism were fuelled continually by the presence of Mary Queen of Scots under house arrest in Derbyshire, guarded by the Earl of Shrewsbury. Her existence also heightened the anxiety of the Council (and Parliament and the people in general) about the succession: Elizabeth had no direct heir and there were many who might support Mary if Elizabeth were to die first. This perpetual worry in turn gave an added dimension to her councillors' personal concern for Elizabeth's health.

In East Anglia, a populous and prosperous area of the kingdom, and particularly in Norfolk and Suffolk, there were a number of important Catholic families who would not give up their old ways. There were also some suspicions that the Bishop of Norwich, Edmund Freake, was disinclined to act against recusants while coming down heavily on Puritanism, the extreme wing of Protestantism, whose adherents wanted further reform of the Church. The Council intended to use the progress to deal with these problems and they set out fully briefed on the identities and locations of dissidents. This was to be more than the usual publicity exercise.

The other major preoccupation of the Council in the summer of 1578 was the situation in the Netherlands. The seventeen provinces belonged to Spain but they had enjoyed a degree of self-government until, in 1567, a Spanish army was sent in to quell the growth of Calvinism, particularly in the north, and since 1572 they had been in revolt. Elizabeth favoured the Protestant cause but was reluctant to support rebels against their rightful sovereign, even Philip of Spain. So, though her councillors wanted action, she vacillated. In 1577 she had actually promised help with men and money and by 20 May 1578 the £20,000 in gold promised to John Casimir had been packed in seventeen chests and, accompanied by four officials, had reached Antwerp. Two days later, however, it was reported that the Dutch were negotiating with the French, and the Queen herself sent instructions that the money was not to be handed over until she was satisfied on the point. In fact, her preference all along was not to become directly involved but to work for a peaceful settlement which would be cheaper on both counts. On 2 June Lord Burghley made a note: 'Peace. To send men authorized of quallitie to move both partyes thereto.'[11]

The men chosen were Lord Cobham and Sir Francis Walsingham, who set out about Sunday 15 June and reached Dunkirk the following Saturday. They took another week to get to Antwerp, their slow progress due apparently to the size of their accompanying party, 120-odd people. Their objective was to bring the Spanish and the Dutch together and to prevent the Duc d'Alençon, younger brother of the King of France, from moving in to help the rebels and so establish the French in the

Low Countries. The Queen's reception of proposals of marriage from Alençon – twenty years her junior and pockmarked – was also, at least partly, designed to control his activities and to ward off a threat to England from whomever controlled the Netherlands coast and more particularly Antwerp, the gateway to Europe for the English cloth trade. Although a Catholic, he was ready to help the Netherlands against Spain and he professed himself willing to be guided by Elizabeth in his actions there. Her councillors were sceptical of his protestations and they saw the position in the Netherlands as a major threat to the safety of the realm. As Lord Sussex wrote on 6 August, 'The case will be hard with the Queen and with England if ever the French possess or the Spaniards tyrannize in the Low Countries.'

The Council also dealt with numerous appeals, complaints and other matters not of national importance. Most of their decisions on particular cases would not have concerned the Queen unless they stemmed from an audience with her, but she would have heard of some of them from one or other of her councillors. It is likely, for example, that she knew of the prisoner in the Tower who claimed to be her half-brother, Edward VI. In fact, a good deal of the Council's time was taken up with judicial matters such as decisions on the fate of prisoners (some of whom they interviewed) and steps to be taken against poachers, smugglers, counterfeiters of coin and occasionally spies. They also dealt with personal appeals for help, often referring them to local magnates to settle. And they were concerned with the raising of troops and their training. In particular, in June they required 1,000 men from the south-west to be sent to Ireland. The Queen had already heard complaints about the behaviour of the English soldiers there; she believed that 'such greavous extorcons suffered uncorrected maketh our government more hatefull to that nacion' and they had to be checked. In contrast, on 8 July, to reduce the state's expenditure, they summoned three navy officials, including Edward Baesh, with whom the Queen had stayed in May, to give orders that no ships were to put to sea and the men were to be dismissed.

Meanwhile, plans for the progress into East Anglia took shape. Already in May the outline was known. Even before the minor progress, Gilbert Talbot reported that 'it is thought that Her Majesty will go in Progress to Norfolk this year but there is no certain determination thereof as yet'.[12] By the middle of June, plans had crystallized sufficiently for Thetford and Norwich to be warned to expect the Queen in August. Later still Thomas Churchyard, a kind of professional impresario to the Court, was sent to Norwich to organize some of the entertainments to be presented before the Queen. He arrived about 25 July and was followed later by others on similar missions.

By this time houses at which she might stay had been inspected by an officer of the Chamber. At some time in the early part of 1578, William Bowles, one of the Yeomen of Her Majesty's Chamber, was due to visit nearly two dozen houses between

Greenwich and north Norfolk as possible stops on 'the way outward'. For 'the way homewards' he was to cover a dozen more, from Brackenash near Norwich to Harrow-on-the-Hill.[13]

In fact, when the progress finally took place, only a handful of the houses inspected were used by the Queen and many were far off the route that was actually taken. Some of the reports might have come in useful the following year, however, when an itinerary was drawn up for the Queen to travel again through Essex and Suffolk (though further to the east than in 1578) and to stay at seven of the places visited by William Bowles. In the event, however, this progress was delayed and curtailed and only two of Bowles's houses were used.

Finally, after the Queen's 'gestes' had been published, a report, based perhaps on Bowles's observations and entitled 'A breef Shew of the Scituacion of the severall howses named in her Majestys jestes wth the nombre of myles betwene every of them',[14] covered a dozen houses about 10 miles apart between Thetford and Harrow, including five of those on Bowles's list, with a sketch map of the possible routes. It also commented on the size, position and outlook of the houses and on the health of the surrounding area.

Early in July, though plans were still quite fluid, the decision to move off had been taken. On 8 July the Council wrote to the Bishop of London, the Lieutenant of the Tower and other commissioners to say that 'her Majesty mindeth to remove into some partes distant from the City of London' but wished it still to be well governed in her absence; 'her pleasure was that they should from to time be assisting to the Lord Maior and officers of the city to see peace and good order'. Their first meeting to discuss their task was held on 18 July at the Lord Mayor's house. It was attended by the Bishop, the Lieutenant, Lord Wentworth and the Recorder of London, William Fletewood. Sir William Cordell, Master of the Rolls, was absent; he may well already have joined the progress.[15]

By now the Gentlemen Ushers were starting out. Three teams began work in July, led by Symon Bowyer and Anthony Wingfeld, who had been with the minor progress, and Piers Pennante. Pennante and Bowyer, each with a team comprising a Yeoman Usher, three Yeomen of the Chamber and two Grooms of the Chamber with two Grooms of the Wardrobe (of beds and other furniture) and a Groom Porter, set off first. They took with them and set up the furniture, put up the hangings and generally created a home from home for the Queen, whether she was travelling to one of her own houses which would have been closed down in her absence or to a house belonging to one of her subjects where they might also appropriate some of the best pieces for their own purposes.

As in May, the officers of the Wardrobe of Robes travelled separately; Charles Smythe, Page of Her Majesty's Robes, who had also been with the minor progress, left London about the same time as the ushers. John Pigion and his man must have

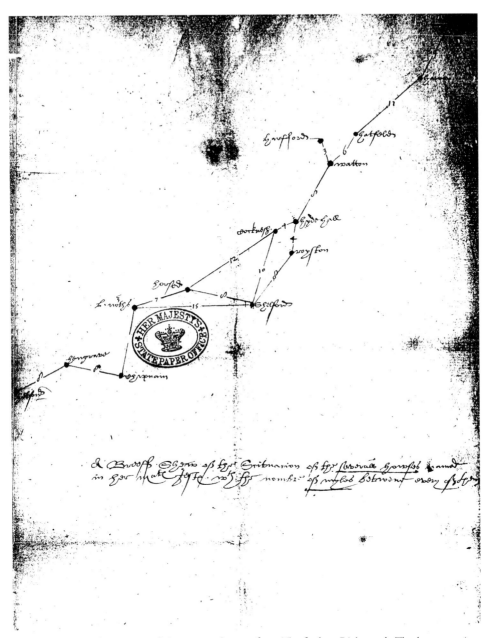

A court official's sketch map of the proposed route from Thetford to Richmond. The last stage (top right) is Harrow to Hampton (PRO SP12/125 f46).

left a little later, taking gold and silver plate for the Queen's use from the Tower of London to her palace at Havering. Finally, two clerks to the Treasurer of the Chamber and their men rode from the City of London, carrying money to wherever it might be needed for 'the dispatche and defrayinge of the paymentes' to be made by their master. They were paid 20s a month between them, which had to include the cost of hiring horses, carts and boats and the extra security required during the progress.

Rather belatedly, on 13 July, the Postmaster of the Court, Thomas Randolph, was instructed by the Council, now at Havering, to 'lay posts' wherever necessary for the conveyance of letters to and from the Court during the progress. (Instructions for him to be paid for this work were not issued until a month later, on 12 August.) His arrangements were evidently effective, for letters passed frequently and swiftly between the Queen and the Council and their agents both within England and abroad.

CHAPTER 2

OVER FAMILIAR GROUND
11 JULY–1 AUGUST

To Havering

The first step of the long journey into the unfamiliar regions of East Anglia was a short move over well-known ways to the royal palace of Havering, where the progress was to halt for more than a week, longer than they were to rest again until they reached Norwich.

When the Queen left Greenwich on Friday 11 July she was accompanied by many of her courtiers, the Chamber officers who had not already gone ahead, her government in the form of a number of her Privy Councillors and all their officials and servants – an immense throng. In addition, she was escorted by the Yeomen of the Guard, a body which had been established in 1485 at Henry VII's accession as a working palace guard. In 1578 they numbered about 130. The entire body accompanied the progress and 'in consideration of the great paines by them then to be taken' their wages for July, August and September were increased from $20d$ to $2s$ $0d$ per day. In 1578 their Captain was Sir Christopher Hatton, the Queen's Vice-Chamberlain.

The Queen's escort also included a band of Gentlemen Pensioners. These were a mounted royal bodyguard created by Henry VIII and used mainly on ceremonial occasions. Unlike the Yeomen, they were not all on duty at the same time; when needed, a dozen or so would be assembled to serve for a limited period. They stood guard inside the presence chamber and were of higher rank (and more expensive) than the Yeomen who were stationed outside. Their distinctive insignia included a heavy gold chain and they carried a halberd, a ceremonial gilt battle-axe topped with a spearhead. Their horsemanship made them expert tilters at royal tournaments.

The Queen and her entourage first crossed the Thames by barge and again probably travelled some way up the River Lea. They may well have landed where the Lea divided and was crossed by a series of bridges. From there on they rode, meeting perhaps at that point or along the way the Yeomen of the Guard and parties of others

The progress into East Anglia (detail from Christopher Saxton's map of England and Wales, 1579, published with his atlas of county maps, 1579). The superimposed route is an indication of direction only; Saxton's maps do not show roads.

who were to accompany them, including, in each county, the sheriff and other local personages. By mid- or late morning the Queen had reached the house of Mr Mewtas in West Ham, where she was to dine. It had been chosen simply as a suitable place for the main meal of the day. Mr Mewtas was not expected to entertain the Queen, though he very likely made some contribution to the meal for the sake of his reputation and future. He was after all a rich man.

The Mewtas estate was based on the former Stratford Abbey, which had been given at the Dissolution by Henry VIII to Sir Peter de Meautis, his ambassador to France and Scotland. De Meautis's grandfather had come from Calais and had served as secretary for French affairs to Henry VII.[1] By 1578 the wealthy Mewtas family was settled in West Ham. The Queen's host was Hercules Mewtas, Sir Peter's son. When he died in 1587, he was buried in West Ham Church, 'where my mother, brother and kindred lie', leaving, among other bequests, a year's wages of 4 marks (4 × 13s 4d) to each of his servants and a pair of falcons and a bay gelding to his executors.[2]

At his house Gentleman Usher Symon Bowyer and his team had created 'a dyninge howse' suitably equipped for the Queen's dinner. For this informal occasion he probably appropriated the Mewtas plate, hangings and furniture. The food and drink, for the accompanying throng of officials and servants, as well as for the Queen, would have been provided in advance by the Royal Household, so the cost to Mr Mewtas lay in any contributions he chose to make and in the considerable upheaval and disruption to his household. Charles Smythe had already prepared 'the office of the roabes' so that the Queen could change out of her travelling clothes if she wished. After the meal, when the Queen had moved on, all their preparations had to be reversed and any equipment which they had brought had to be taken down and carried away. All this took Symon Bowyer two days and Charles Smythe one.

That night the Queen was settled at her own palace of Havering, about 10 miles to the north-east. Havering was an old medieval palace which had been altered and extended from time to time. Additional accommodation had been added in the two years before this visit and some renovation work was still going on even after the Queen's arrival. It continued until 22 July under the supervision of Thomas Fowler, Controller of Works, who had checked the security of the houses on the minor progress. At Havering his work included 'makinge of the boylinghouse [where large joints of meat were cooked before being prepared for the table] . . . making furnisses for the boylinghouse and scullery', as well as 'mending olde cubbordes, tables, dores, gates, pales and staires' and 'makinge a seatt in the garden'.[3]

The Queen's suite of rooms on the first floor was on the standard pattern which the Gentlemen Ushers had to create at all the private houses where she stayed. A large presence chamber, 40 ft long, led into the slightly smaller privy chamber, which in turn led into the withdrawing chamber; beyond was the bedchamber, 22 ft by 12½ ft, set in an angle of the building. A passage outside led to a stair down to the rooms of the Ladies of the Bedchamber. No major works were carried out in the next twenty years and a survey of the palace made in 1596 listed nearly fifty rooms. Five of the largest were taken up by the royal suite, there were two chapels and the Lord Chamberlain and his wife had their own rooms. Another on the ground floor was set aside for Lord Treasurer Burghley. Most of the rest, such as the kitchens, the larder, the buttery and the cellars, housed domestic services, the servants sleeping in and around their work.[4]

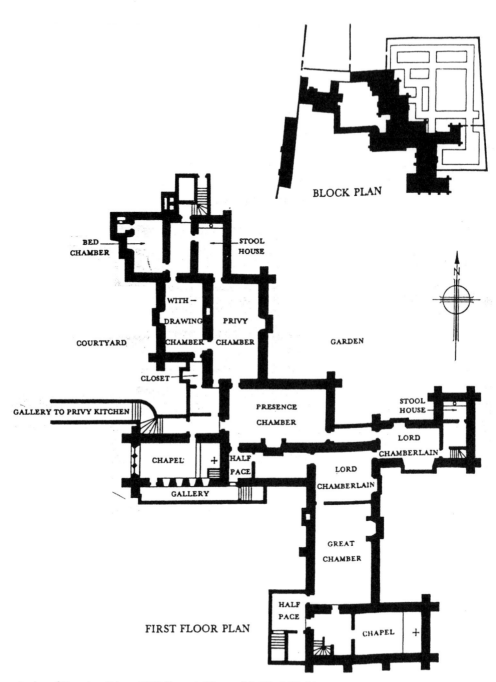

A plan of Havering Palace, 1578 (from *A History of the King's Works*).

A second team under Gentleman Usher Piers Pennante spent six days setting up and taking down the furnishings of the royal apartments; and Charles Smythe, who had spent one day at West Ham, came to Havering for three days to serve in the Wardrobe of Robes. His offices and stores were on the ground floor below the Queen's private rooms. John Pigion from the Jewel House also arrived, bringing the silver plate.

This progress was not a holiday for anyone. Affairs of state had to be dealt with as usual and Council meetings were held at Havering on six days, including the two Sundays, between 12 and 20 July. They were attended by the small nucleus of members who were to appear regularly throughout the progress: Lord Burghley, Lord Treasurer and the Queen's chief minister of state; the Earl of Sussex, the Lord Chamberlain, chief officer of the Chamber; Sir Christopher Hatton, the Vice-Chamberlain, his deputy; Sir Francis Knollys, Treasurer of the Household; Sir James Croft, Controller of the Household; the Earl of Warwick, Master of Ordnance (Ambrose Dudley, brother of Lord Leicester); and Dr Thomas Wilson, Secretary of State. At three meetings they were joined by the Lord Admiral, the Earl of Lincoln, Lord Steward, chief officer of the Queen's Household, who on this occasion did not stay with the progress, and at two by Lord Hunsdon.

As usual, wherever the Council was based, couriers came and went, the movements of many reflecting the Council's prime interest in foreign affairs. Between 12 and 17 July one arrived from the ambassadors in the Netherlands and two from Paris. One of these was on the staff of the English ambassador in Paris, Sir Amyas Paulet. He arrived on Saturday 12 July and left again on the following Wednesday, when the Council authorized payment of his expenses for 'beinge lately imployed in the service of Her Majesty beyonde the seas'. Two other men left for Ireland, one of them taking sixteen cartloads of munitions and artillery.

As for the Council's judicial responsibilities at home, two parties brought in prisoners to be examined. Among their minor concerns were the case of a man long imprisoned in the Tower who was at last to be released, subject to appearing before them with fourteen days' notice, and measures to protect the Queen's printer from his competitors. On 13 July they issued the orders, already mentioned, for the conveyance of their mail while they were on the move.

On the Saturday, the day after they had arrived at Havering, messengers brought the Council news of a sinister-seeming meeting of conspirators late the previous night. An envoy from King Henri III of France, on a mission to visit Mary Queen of Scots, had been discovered by the watch in conference with two Englishmen, Sir William Morgan and Sir Warham St Leger, late at night in a dark tree-covered area on the south bank of the Thames. Reports of events that Friday night were sent to Burghley at Theobalds (mistakenly) and to Sir Christopher Hatton at Havering by William Fletewood, Recorder of London and one of those charged with the good government of London in the Queen's absence. His instructions reached him on the Saturday night and Recorder Fletewood spent a busy twenty-four hours. By Monday 13 July he had located the conspirators, taken statements from the watermen who had ferried the parties concerned and from the Southwark watch, and had sent back a full report to Havering. No more was heard of this 'plot' and no action seems to have been taken against the two Englishmen. Perhaps the Recorder had over-reacted on the first night of the Council's absence from London.[5]

Lord Leicester, as Master of the Horse – a position he held from Elizabeth's accession in 1558 until his death thirty years later – completed the regular group of councillors. He was still at Buxton Spa, but by 9 July, as he wrote to Hatton, although he had 'found great ease by this bath', he was anxious to return to the Court. He thought, wrongly, that the Queen was due to visit Wanstead again, presumably on her way to Havering, and was troubled 'not a little' that he could not get there to receive her. Nevertheless, he was determined to 'hie me home' and rejoin the Queen as soon as he could: 'I hope now ere long to be with you to enjoy that blessed sight which I have been so long kept from. A few of these days seem many years.'[6]

He reached Havering on 19 July, to the Queen's evident satisfaction. Richard Topclyffe, writing to his patron Lord Shrewsbury, who owned the Spa, reported that she was enjoying her travels now that Leicester was with her and intended to thank him and Lady Shrewsbury (the redoubtable Bess of Hardwick) for his restored health.[7] By the next day Leicester had evidently taken stock of the international situation and found it alarming. Never, he wrote to Walsingham, in the dramatic style of the times, had the Crown been in greater peril or the Queen in greater need of reliable men around her.

Lord Leicester had a special position vis-à-vis the Queen but all the close inner group of councillors were personally, as well as politically, attached to her. Nevertheless, their loyalty was sorely tried from time to time by her procrastination and changeability. The day before Leicester arrived she had been particularly difficult. The ambassadors in the Low Countries had forwarded a request, which the Council had supported, for further financial help from England for the Dutch. Lord Burghley reported her reaction, more in resignation than complaint. His messenger would be able to tell the ambassadors, he said, 'how sharp Her Majesty has been with some of us here'. The Council endured her censures in the knowledge that 'however she mislikes things at one time, at another she will alter her sharpness especially when she is persuaded that we all mean truly for her safety – though she sometimes will not so understand'. He signed his letter from Havering, 'where I am kept only to receive some chidings upon daily debate of these matters'. No wonder he took a little time off a day or two later.

The Queen stayed at Havering for ten days, three or four days longer than planned.

Perhaps because of this, some people were confused about her intentions. On 18 July Sir Nicholas Bacon, Lord Keeper of the Great Seal, was not sure whether the Queen would continue her progress from Essex into Suffolk and on the following day the Earl of Northumberland sent a messenger from London to Lord Burghley at Havering to inquire about it.[8]

Eventually, however, they moved on and the progress fell into a familiar pattern which was to last for the next two months. The heavy baggage train had already gone ahead, the Gentlemen Ushers followed and the main party arrived at the next destination to find all ready.

To Standon

The Queen left Havering early on Monday 21 July and again stopped for dinner at a convenient house roughly half-way to her next lodging. This was Garnish Hall, Theydon Garnon, the home of Alderman John Branch, a wealthy London merchant, later to be Lord Mayor of London and in 1581 knighted. He had married a rich heiress, Ellen Hampden, through whom he acquired the manor of Theydon Garnon. She died in 1567 and he remarried; his second wife was also called Ellen.[9] At his house, Piers Pennante, coming from Havering, spent two days on another 'dynner house'. The arrangements were probably much the same as at West Ham. Raphe Hope, Yeoman of Her Majesty's Wardrobe of Robes, joined the progress to replace Charles Smythe, who had gone back to Greenwich for more things. He and his two men spent one day at Garnish Hall.

After the meal the journey continued and by nightfall the Queen was at 'Mr Altam's', Mark Hall, Latton, now part of Harlow. James Altam, another wealthy London merchant, had already entertained the Queen for a few days in September 1571 and overnight in 1576. Earlier in his career he had been an Alderman of the City of London but he had failed in his duties and in 1561 was deprived of his office and fined. The following year he bought Mark Hall and lived there from then on. He became a diligent Essex Justice and in 1571 he was made Sheriff, but he never achieved a knighthood. He had married as his second wife Dame Mary Judd, the widow of a former Lord Mayor of London, who continued to be called by her title since her previous husband – her third – was of higher rank than Mr Altam. Even in his will she is called 'the Lady Judd my loving wife'. From their previous marriages he had five children and she nine. When he died in 1583, she put up a very handsome monument to him in St Mary-at-Latton Church. She died in 1602, aged eighty-five, and was buried in the same tomb. In her will one room in the house was still referred to as 'the Queen's chamber'.

Leaving Havering and Theydon Garnon to Piers Pennante, Symon Bowyer and his team spent six days at Mark Hall and Raphe Hope came directly from Theydon

Monument to James Altham and his wife, Lady Judd, in St Mary-at-Latton Church, Harlow. The kneeling children are probably her two sons and seven daughters by three earlier husbands. The verses below them begin

Here lyes a lady full of fruitfull age
Blest in large seed and forefold marriage.

Garnon for three. The house was large – though the great majority of the Queen's followers would have had to be accommodated in the surrounding area – and very comfortably furnished with feather beds, woollen blankets, fine linen sheets and pillowcases and silk curtains. There were bedcovers in velvet and satin, embroidered and tapestry cushions and Turkey carpets on the tables and cupboards. There were two great chairs, though most people sat on stools or in the cushioned windowseats. The table was covered with linen cloths and equipped with napkins and a great range of silver and silver-gilt plates, bowls, spoons, goblets, salts and a chafing dish. The Court officers would have had no difficulty in creating appropriate quarters for the Queen.[10]

The Court was settled there in time for Secretary Wilson to reply to a letter from the ambassadors in the Netherlands which he had received that morning at Havering; it had come from Antwerp in only three days. Wilson had 'a matter of great moment' to tell them which they were to handle 'with all dexterity'. It had been reported by other sources that the Duc d'Alençon had moved into the Low Countries in response to an offer of marriage with his daughter from the Protestant leader, William of Orange – this in spite of Alençon's wooing of the Queen with the backing of the French royal family. Such double dealing 'cannot but seem very strange and give sufficient cause of just offence'. Sir Francis Walsingham was to seek the truth from both parties. The courier taking the letter set off at once.

Lord Burghley usually travelled with the Queen, dealing with affairs of state as he went. However, for a few days now, probably with some relief, he went to his own house, Theobalds, about 10 miles away, missing the Council meeting held at Mark Hall on 23 July, at which only some comparatively minor matters of domestic concern were discussed, and another at Standon on 24 July.

While he was at Theobalds he received another report on various dubious activities noted by the ever-vigilant Recorder of London. Among those whose movements had been watched was the wife of Sir William Morgan, one of the south-bank conspirators. She had been seen at night approaching Sackville Place, the home of Lord Buckhurst, where the suspect French envoy was lodged. On investigation, however, it turned out that she had simply called on Lady Buckhurst and then gone on to visit her mother, the same Lady Judd with whom the Queen was then staying. Perhaps Lady Morgan was anxious to take the opportunity to present a loyal face before the Queen.[11]

On 21 July Burghley wrote from Theobalds to Thomas Randolph, the Court Post Master, who was escorting an envoy from King James VI of Scotland to the Queen. James at this time was twelve years old. His regent, Morton, had England's support but in March he had been temporarily ousted by a group of rival earls and recovered his position only in June. On 1 July he had written to Lord Burghley advising him that the Lord of Dunfermline, ambassador from the King to Her Majesty, would arrive shortly. A few days later Sir Francis Walsingham in the Netherlands, having already heard this news, thought that Dunfermline was looking for 'closer amity between the two Crowns' but that the Queen was likely to show more reluctance than was safe, 'considering how much it imparts with her [is important for her] to be sure of that Crown and what mislike it will breed in case upon the overture it should be refused'. Events were to show how well he knew his Queen.

The Scottish ambassador had travelled first to London, evidently missing the departure of the progress, so the Lord Mayor was sent instructions from the Council at Havering to arrange accommodation for him, 'a man of good credit sent out of Scotland to Her Majesty'. Accordingly he was lodged in Fenchurch Street until he could set off again in pursuit of the Queen.[12] Thomas Randolph, deputed to escort him, seems not to have relished his job. He was, he said, 'not unwilling to do anything I am charged though I could have wished that some other man had had that office'.[13]

Burghley invited them both to dine with him on Thursday 24 July, when he would be able to show Randolph his new house. He added modestly that, considering his foreign travels, Randolph would not see much to please him, except perhaps in comparison with 'Muscovia' (he had been in Russia ten years earlier). In fact, when Theobalds was finished in 1585, it was considered the finest house in England.[14]

Lord Hunsdon was to join them and the envoy was to stay at his house that night, going on to Sir Raphe Sadler's on 25 July. Hunsdon House had been a royal palace built by Henry VIII but mostly used by his children. Elizabeth had given it to her cousin Henry Carey, the son of her aunt Mary, Anne Boleyn's sister. He was a popular soldier figure and in 1559 she had made him Lord Hunsdon.[15] He attended a number of Council meetings at this time but left the progress after Audley End when he was ordered to the Scottish border.

The next move, probably on 23 July, was made without a prearranged stop for dinner. Probably the Queen's departure from Latton was delayed until after the morning meal or perhaps she reached Standon in Hertfordshire in time for dinner – Sir Raphe Sadler's house was only about 9 miles away. Here the third Gentleman Usher, Anthony Wingfeld, and his nine-man team spent six days and Raphe Hope three. John Pigion from the Jewel House also arrived at Standon with the plate, probably brought on from Havering. The Queen had previously stayed there in 1561 on her way back from Ipswich; this time she stayed three days.

Sir Raphe, now seventy-one, had been a faithful servant of the Protestant Tudor monarchy for many years and had been knighted by Henry VIII. (Under Mary Tudor he had retired quietly to Standon.) In 1568 Elizabeth had made him Chancellor of the Duchy of Lancaster and he became a trusted agent of Lord Burghley. His duties brought him into contact with Mary Queen of Scots intermittently throughout her life. He had first seen her as a baby when he reported on her health and strength to Henry VIII, he had been her guardian in 1572 during her long imprisonment in

England (and would be again between 1584 and 1585) and he was to attend her trial in 1586. Early in life he had married a woman whose first husband, thought to have died abroad, was found to be still alive; eventually an Act of Parliament in 1546 made their seven children legitimate. After his death in 1587, aged eighty, a magnificent monument was erected to him in Standon Church.

Sir Raphe attended the Council meeting held at his house on 24 July and another at Audley End on 29 July. Among the Council's business at Standon was a report that the Sheriff of Pembrokeshire had delayed the execution of a condemned murderer. They issued orders that the execution was to be carried out and that the Sheriff himself was to appear before them within fourteen days. Presumably the courier who carried their letter was able to tell the Sheriff how to find the Council on their travels. Other couriers arrived from Antwerp, one having come via Paris; another from Scotland went straight back; and another returned to his post in Ireland.

The Scottish ambassador, arriving on 25 July, reached Standon before the Court left and may have begun his talks with the Council there. He certainly accompanied or followed them on the next stage of the progress.

To Audley End

The Queen left Standon on Saturday 26 July. On her way to Audley End, a distance of about 15 miles, she had dinner at Berden Priory, just into Essex. The former Augustinian priory at Berden had been acquired by Thomas Averey from a previous owner in 1553.[16] Thomas had died in 1576, leaving his property to his wife, Mary. He also left £6 13s 4d to 'a boie called John Averey' to be paid within two months of his death. He and Mary had no living children of their own and the boy John was not related to them but lived in the household as one of the family, bearing the name of his benefactor. Indeed he was to inherit the estate after Mary's death.[17] In the meantime, it was in her house that Wingfeld spent two days and Raphe Hope one, both coming on about 6 miles or so from Standon. Mistress Averey was probably one of those householders who were required to provide only a clean, empty house before the arrival of the Court officers to get it ready.

At Audley End it was Symon Bowyer and his team, arriving from Mark Hall, who came for the six days. Both Wardrobe of Robes officers attended, perhaps because of the importance of the Queen's engagements there. Raphe Hope, who had already worked on the four previous houses, took four days for his work and some stocktaking seems to have gone on. Charles Smythe, last recorded at Havering, arrived back from London with 'divers necessaries' and one of Bowyer's team, 'Yeoman of Her Majesty's Warde Roabes of Beddes', returned to Greenwich. The 'wardrobe stuffe' he collected was carried up to London by boat and brought by cart to the Court, which by then had reached Long Melford; he was paid 16s 8d.

Elizabeth, Lady Audley, c. 1538 (Hans Holbein the Younger).

Her daughter, Margaret, second wife of the 4th Duke of Norfolk (detail, Rebecca Biagio, after Hans Eworth).

Audley End was then the property of Thomas Howard, second son of the 4th Duke of Norfolk, who had been executed just a year after the Queen's previous visit to the house in 1571, when he was already under house arrest in London. Young Thomas's mother, Margaret, the Duke's second wife, was the daughter and sole heir of Thomas Audley, Henry VIII's Lord Chancellor, who had been granted the Benedictine abbey of Walden at the time of the Dissolution of the Monasteries and from it had created his house. Margaret, whose portrait still hangs in the Great Hall, died in 1564, aged twenty-four, leaving the house to her elder son, then two and a half, who had been born there. When she died, her mother, Lady Audley, took charge of the Duke's five children, all under seven, until their father remarried three years later.[18] After his arrest, the family was removed from their father's palace of Kenninghall (where the progress was to halt a couple of weeks later) to Audley End; they were escorted by Sir Nicholas Lestrange, his Chamberlain.[19]

When the Queen came, Thomas was just under seventeen and played no part in the occasion. Later he was to follow his uncle Charles of Effingham to sea and was knighted for gallantry against the Armada. He was made Lord Howard de Walden after the capture of Cadiz in 1596 and later still he was created Earl of Suffolk by James I. In 1605 he led the search of the Westminster cellars which exposed the Gunpowder Plot. He replaced his grandfather's house with an immense palace built between 1603 and 1614.

Earlier in the month, before he left Havering, Lord Burghley, who was Chancellor of the University of Cambridge, had been consulted by the Vice-Chancellor about a proposed delegation to the Queen while she was at Audley End, where she was expected to be on 22 July.[20] In reply he recommended that the gloves to be given as presents to Lord Leicester and others should be accompanied by appropriate verses. The book for the Queen would also be acceptable, provided it had not been perfumed by the bookbinder, as was common, for the Queen could not stand a strong scent.

He also reported that the Queen intended to delay her departure from Havering, so her arrival at Audley End would be later than expected. Indeed, after Long Melford she might turn back towards London via Cambridge (in the event, of course, the progress was not cut short). Not surprisingly, the arrangements for the university visit could not be settled for another ten days, when the progress had moved on. By Friday 25 July Burghley had rejoined the Queen at Standon and was able to let the Vice-Chancellor know that it was now certain she would be at Audley End the following night. Final details would be sent then; meanwhile, he was able to advise that they should come in their long black gowns. In fact, a messenger from Cambridge reached the Court while they were still halted for dinner at Berden on the Saturday. He returned with instructions signed by both Burghley and Leicester to come to Audley End the following morning; the Cambridge party would be presented to the Queen in the afternoon.[21]

So on Sunday 27 July the Vice-Chancellor and the college heads arrived. When they had been brought into the Queen's presence, Mr Bridgewater of King's College gave an oration in Latin. Then the Vice-Chancellor, Mr Howland of St John's, presented the Queen with a New Testament in Greek, bound in red velvet and decorated with gold and enamel, and a pair of perfumed and embroidered gloves. Fourteen others also received gloves; the Queen's cost 60*s*, Lord Burghley's and Lord Leicester's were 20*s* and Lord Sussex's 4*s* 2*d*. The others given gloves included three members of the Howard family: Philip, Earl of Surrey, Thomas's older half-brother, who was to entertain the Queen at his own houses in Norfolk; Charles of Effingham, one of Thomas's uncles, and later to be the naval commander against the Armada; and Henry, later to be Earl of Northampton, another uncle. Attached were verses punning on their mottoes and crests and decorated with their arms. The university was evidently well informed about the royal party and had worked swiftly to produce appropriate gifts. No mention is made of Thomas himself; he was, after all, still a minor.

The weather that day was hot and after the oration the Queen withdrew to her own rooms. The visitors moved to Lord Leicester's quarters and, after refreshments in the form of beer and wine, they held a 'Disputation of Philosophy' on Mercy versus Severity in a prince. Burghley had earlier expressed some doubts about a second subject suggested by the Vice-Chancellor and it may have been modified or omitted altogether. This was whether or not the stars could affect men's lives and reflected the general interest of the time in astrology. In any case, it was Burghley who chaired the debate, refusing to allow repetitions and limiting the length of speeches. Even so, it lasted over three hours. The party finally left for Cambridge about midnight, there being nowhere for them to stay in Saffron Walden, where no doubt the inns were already doing good business.[22]

Among those taking part in the debate was Gabriel Harvey of Pembroke College (former tutor and lifelong friend of the poet Edmund Spenser), who presented Burghley with four pages of Latin verses written in his own hand and addressed to the Queen, Lord Leicester and Lord Burghley among others.

Before they left, Harvey and some of the Queen's followers went over to Henry Bradbury's house at Littlebury, less than 2 miles away, which had been taken into use by the Court officers. They went to call on Margaret, Lady Derby, one of the Queen's ladies, who was lodged there while the progress halted at Audley End.[23] Lady Derby was the granddaughter of Henry VIII's sister Mary, who, after the death of her first husband, King Louis XII of France, had married Henry's close friend Charles Brandon, Duke of Suffolk; Margaret's mother was a child of this marriage. Her husband, Henry, Earl of Derby, also had Tudor connections, being descended from Margaret Beaufort, mother of Henry VII. Lady Derby had been one of the Queen's ladies since early in the reign and Elizabeth liked to have her at Court, where she could keep an eye on a possible claimant

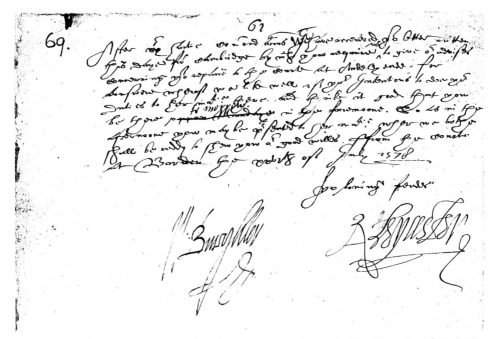

Hurried letter from Lord Burghley and Lord Leicester at Berden to the Vice-Chancellor of Cambridge University. They 'thinke it good that you be there tomorrow ['uppon Mondaye' crossed out] in the forenoone. So as in the afternoon you may be presented to her ma[jes]tie wher we both shall be reddy to show you our good willes' (Cambridge University Library UA Lett 9 f69).

to the throne. Nevertheless, she was kind to her distant relative, who was continually in debt and in dispute with her husband, whose allowance did not meet her bills. Both the Queen and the Council tried to help her, Elizabeth even arranging for her to have lodgings at Court to save her expense. Debts or no, Lady Derby's New Year gifts to the Queen were often rich things to wear; at the beginning of 1578, she had presented a white satin petticoat with a broad edge of multicoloured embroidery and the next year it was to be a tawny velvet gown.

Her favoured position was to change sharply the following summer when in August the Duc d'Alençon came in person to woo Elizabeth. He arrived incognito and stayed only ten days, officially in secret. Of course, everyone at Court knew he was there, but they had to pretend otherwise. Lady Derby, however, was heard gossiping about his presence and was immediately banned from Court and placed under house arrest. Her fault was compounded by allegations that she had consulted a magician to find out how long Elizabeth would live. The Queen did not readily forgive her and she was still exiled from Court a year later, though grateful to be allowed to live first in a kinsman's house and then in her own at Isleworth, and not in the Tower, as had been threatened at first.[24]

On the Monday another courtier joined the progress. This was Lord North, riding from his home, Kirtling in Cambridgeshire, about 15 miles to the north, where the Queen was to stop on her return journey in exactly five weeks' time. He brought with him his son and heir, John, aged about twenty-two, who, having been introduced at Court, returned home the same night. He had evidently been given permission to return, for he was to appear at intervals throughout the next month. John must have intended to make a fine show at Court and on the previous Monday he and his brother Henry had ridden to London on a shopping expedition. His purchases were mainly clothes and accessories, but he also bought songbooks and had his lute and his swords mended. By far his biggest single outlay, 12s, was on sweetmeats, probably to be gifts to some of the people he would meet. For the six days he was away, including overnight stops at Saffron Walden and Hoddesdon and his party's upkeep in London (where they would have lodged at the family's Charterhouse home), the total cost was £5 4s 2d.[25]

There is no record of gifts given to the Queen at Audley End, but some people who were involved in the visit are mentioned in the next annual Court list of New Year gifts. 'Lord Howard' (probably Charles of Effingham) gave her 'a locke of golde black enamuled sett wth xvi smale diamonds' and Lord Henry Howard (Northampton) 'a juell of golde being a dead tree with mistiltowe wth smale sparckes of dyamondes and rubyes at the roote'.[26]

Saffron Walden's gifts were more prosaic. During her stay the Guild of Holy Trinity presented the Queen with a silver-gilt cup costing £14 plus 18s for engraving it and 4s for its case. Another £6 12s 4d went on gifts to others in the party, including 5s for 'the carriar of the Quene's robes', presumably Raphe Hope. The resident French ambassador to England, the Sieur de Mauvissière de Castelnau, who had come direct from London to join the progress at Audley End after the departure of his wife for France on 22 July, received a gallon of wine costing 2s. Lord Leicester got a sugar loaf at 17s 8d. In all, the Guild spent £22 13s on the visit, £6 13s 6d less than in 1571.

Early expenses had included 1s 8d for wine at the White Hart for 'three of the Garde that came to see the state of the town', possibly William Bowles's party (Audley End was on his list). The Guild also gave the Queen's Clerk of the Market 10s and paid for his supper at the White Hart and for fodder for his three horses. The prices he set for supplies to the Court were proclaimed by the Queen's Trumpeter; his tip was 6s 8d.[27]

The Council had nine meetings during their stay at Audley End, the last four on 31 July, just before they moved on. By 27 July Lord Burghley had rejoined the progress, Lord Leicester was attending most meetings and some of the other members

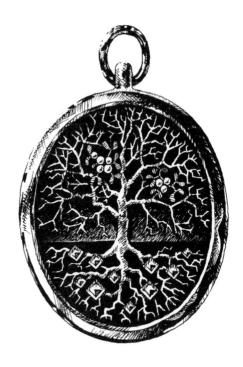

Lord Henry Howard's 1579 New Year gift (artist's impression).

rather fewer. Among their domestic preoccupations were various problems of piracy and the fates of particular prisoners. These last included a married couple caught trying to leave the country clandestinely; the husband was to be examined by Richard Topclyffe, the arch-enemy of Catholics and authorized torturer, if he was in London. (Fortunately, he was with the progress through Suffolk and Norfolk and went on to Burghley House, near Stamford.)

Foreign affairs continued to absorb them. Couriers travelled to and from Antwerp, sometimes via Paris, and to Scotland and Ireland. On 29 July Burghley wrote that the two representatives of the Duc d'Alençon had arrived in London and would reach the Court, which would still be at Audley End, the next day. Earlier in the month, Alençon had written to Elizabeth himself, telling her that he was sending her his Counsellor and Chamberlain in Ordinary, the Sieur de Bacqueville, 'to give her every assurance of his affection that she can possibly desire'. (No wonder she was offended by the reports that he might be going to marry the Orange princess.)

In fact, the arrival of Alençon's envoy had been known at Court for some days. The English ambassador in Paris had reported on 17 July that de Bacqueville would leave in two days' time and by 26 July Secretary Wilson at Standon knew that he had landed at Dover the day before – intelligence travelled fast. De Bacqueville was accompanied by Monsieur de Quissé and four or five young followers of Alençon. One of the Queen's Gentlemen Ushers, Richard Brackenbury, was appointed to escort them, an assignment which lasted nearly two months.

Ambassador Mauvissière had apparently already begun preparing the ground for their arrival. Burghley had learned that he had raised the matter of marriage during 'some conference lately with Her Majesty' at which he himself had not been present.

The Scottish ambassador also had talks with the Council at Audley End. He had come from Standon with the Court on 26 July and that evening Mr Secretary Wilson wrote that he hoped the ambassador would have the answer he wanted within a few days. He remained of this opinion on 29 July, still hoping that James VI's position would be acknowledged. The Council was to consider 'Commendator Dunfermlinge's' plea for support for James that morning and would seek the Queen's view. In the event, they concluded that the question must be settled by the Queen herself, but Dunfermline had to wait for his audience with her until they reached Melford Hall.

Amid all their state business, councillors occasionally received some personal mail. At the end of July a member of Lord Leicester's personal staff sent him some clothes, 'two dublettes' and 'one paire of boote hosen', and samples of patterned velvet for his new nightgown. The accompanying letter also discussed how his new riding cloak might be trimmed.[28] Another personal message went to Lord Cobham in the Low Countries in Wilson's dispatch to Davison about de Bacqueville's arrival. Lady Cobham, who had long been a close friend of the Queen and whose daughter was later to marry Lord Burghley's son Robert, was with the progress; 'she attends diligently and is in health'.

CHAPTER 3

INTO THE UNKNOWN
1–16 AUGUST

To Melford Hall

So far the Queen had travelled through areas with which she and her Court were comparatively familiar. After Audley End, however, she moved into the more distant parts of East Anglia where she had not been before – and would not go again – and where there were few great houses to receive her. From then on, until she was well into the return journey, her hosts were mainly country gentlemen, important in their localities but with little or no experience of the eminent personages who were briefly to take over their houses. Some were or had been MPs, but their chief importance lay in the Council's reliance on local leaders such as the Justices of the Peace to carry out their policies. They were based sufficiently far from the centres of national life to find a visit by the Queen and her Court an exciting experience, but they were also to find that an invasion by the Court and its servants brought its penalties in discomfort to themselves and their households and damage and depredations to their property – not to mention the possible dangers from the Council's scrutiny of their religious inclinations.

Elizabeth probably left Audley End on Friday 1 August, making for Melford Hall, her next major lodging, about 20 miles away. This would involve two days' travelling, but the need to find her suitable houses to pause in on the way extended her journey to almost 25 miles – and provided an opportunity to honour three wealthy local Protestants.

Her first stop was for dinner at the house of Robert Millicent, who lived at Barham Priory near Linton in south-east Cambridgeshire. Robert's father, John, an ardent Protestant, had made a fortune as a government agent during the Dissolution of the Monasteries. He had bought the land of a former priory some twenty-five years earlier and had constructed his house from its buildings, inserting massive oaken doorways and great new windows. John Millicent died in 1577 and is commemorated in St

Mary's Church in a chapel which the family built on to the north aisle; their doorway into it is dated 1587. Robert, his heir, set great store by the family's modern house with its 'waynscott portalls and glasse in the windowes' and took steps to see that they were not removed after his death.[1] Usher Symon Bowyer and his men, coming from Audley End, prepared a 'dininge house at Mr Millesentes' and Charles Smythe, the Wardrobe officer, spent one day at 'Lenton'. Like Mrs Averey, Mr Millicent probably had little to do but let them get on with it.

After dinner the Queen crossed into Suffolk. Her arrival and her reception there were described in detail by Churchyard. He was already in Norwich, having reached there three weeks before she was due to arrive on 16 August, but he had a professional interest in the entertainments offered en route and recorded as much as he could discover from people who were there. He commented that Norfolk and Suffolk had 'small warning' of the Queen's coming but their preparations were extensive: 'All the velvets and silkes were taken up that might be layde hand on and bought for any money.' As usual when she crossed a county boundary, the Queen was met by the Sheriff. William Spring was accompanied by 'two hundred yong gentlemen cladde all in white velvet and three hundred of the graver sorte apparelled in blacke velvet coates and faire chaynes . . . with fifteene hundred serving men more on horsebacke'. There was 'such sumptuous feasting and bankets as seldom in any part of the world hath bin seene before'.

The Queen seems to have been favourably impressed by her reception. Eighty years later, the pastor of the Church of Christ in Lavenham said in a sermon preached at Stowmarket that he had heard how Elizabeth had noticed that the gentlemen of the county who came to meet her were accompanied by their parish priests. 'Now', she said, 'I have learned why my County of Suffolk is so well governed, it is because the magistrates and Ministers go together.'[2]

Her first stop in Suffolk was at the house of Thomas Barnardiston of Kedington, about 3 miles north-east of Haverhill, which Anthony Wingfeld had prepared for her. He had come on from Standon and Berden and, exceptionally, he spent only four days there. Charles Smythe, however, came for three. Probably only Lord Burghley could be found accommodation with the Queen. Lord Leicester, whose whereabouts were usually noted if he and the Queen were parted, stayed at Blunts Hall, another house belonging to Barnardiston a mile or so away.[3]

The Barnardistons were a long-established and wealthy local Protestant family. Rich men of the time liked to decorate their windows, both external and internal, with coloured glass heraldic shields and badges proclaiming their ancestry and family connections; the Barnardiston pedigree was displayed in the parlour windows.[4] When his father died in 1551, the young Thomas Barnardiston became the ward of Sir John Cheke, the Cambridge classical scholar and humanist who had been tutor to Edward VI and Elizabeth when they were children. During the reign of Mary Tudor Thomas was sent to Geneva for safety and no doubt to be brought up in the new religion. In

Tomb of Sir Thomas Barnardiston and his first wife, Elizabeth, in St Peter and St Paul's Church, Kedington, Suffolk. He is in armour; she wears an Elizabethan cap, her head resting on a tasselled cushion. Both have typically Elizabethan ruffs (though he did not die until 1619).

recognition of his religious reliability, when the Queen reached Bury St Edmunds a few days later he was among those who received knighthoods. He married twice and had more than a dozen children. He died in 1619 and was buried in Kedington Church, where a number of his family are also recorded.[5]

The next morning young John North reappeared at Court in time to move on with the progress, arriving with them at Melford in the evening and returning home to Kirtling only when the Queen left.[6] Meanwhile, Elizabeth had stopped for dinner at Colte Hall near Cavendish, in the 'dininge house' prepared by Anthony Wingfeld; her Wardrobe yeoman, Raphe Hope, also spent the day there. The owner, George Colte, was an even wealthier local man. His father had died the previous year leaving him, in addition to the residue of his estate, 'my olde gray mare'; her latest foal, however, was to go to 'Anthonye my Fool'.[7] The medieval custom of retaining in the household a simple person or a dwarf as a personal servant survived into the sixteenth century and to have his own horse must have been a great joy to Anthony. While the Queen was in Colte's house, she knighted her host, rewarding a conformist rather than an enthusiast for the Protestant religion.

Melford Hall, Suffolk, with its six towers (watercolour by Michael Angelo Rooker, 1743–1801).

Melford Hall, which the progress reached that Saturday evening, was the house of Sir William Cordell, Master of the Rolls. He was a local man who had made his fortune as a lawyer and rose to eminence through the reigns of four sovereigns. By 1547 Henry VIII had granted him the manor of Melford, which had previously belonged to the abbey of Bury St Edmunds. Under Mary Tudor he had become Solicitor General and Speaker of the House of Commons. She made him Master of the Rolls in 1557 and he was knighted in 1558. When Elizabeth became Queen, she confirmed his position. He had begun building Melford Hall in the 1550s and by 1578 was getting on in years. His two sons and two daughters had all died in childhood, so he had no direct heir to inherit the great house.[8]

According to Churchyard, Sir William Cordell set the standard for Suffolk hospitality when the progress came and many others were glad to follow his example, entertaining members of the Court if not the Queen herself, presenting gifts and putting on 'triumphes and devises'. Sir William's gifts to Elizabeth, probably presented as she left Melford, were 'a cup of golde, the cover and foote enamuled with eight course diamonds and in the top of the cover a fair emeraude and another cup of golde enameled like thother emerald'.[9] He died three years later and was buried in Long Melford Church, where his tomb seems to include a head of Bacchus as well as the more conventional figures of Temperance, Prudence, Justice and Fortitude.

The length and importance of the Queen's stay were reflected in the official preparations for it. Symon Bowyer, last seen at Audley End and Linton, spent six days making his usual arrangements and another two on 'a bankettinge house'. The 'banquet' was the last, dessert, course of an important meal, when fruit, sweets and decorative confections of sugar paste were served in a separate room or a special small building outside the main house. Bowyer and his men would have put up either a tented pavilion or a structure of branches and flowers in the garden where a few favoured personalities such as the foreign guests of the progress would be invited to join the Queen.

Raphe Hope came from Cavendish and spent three days at Melford, but then he was sent back to Westminster for a gown and 'other necessaries' for the Queen, a trip which took five days. He was to catch up with the Court again at Euston.

On Sunday 3 August Elizabeth gave two important audiences. The French ambassador and Alençon's envoy, Monsieur de Bacqueville, who had arrived as expected, spent a long time with her. The Scottish ambassador also now had his audience with the Queen. Although she presented him with a gold chain,[10] the outcome was disappointing: 'so far was he from getting any relief that he himself went away without any reward'. Walsingham's fears about the Queen's personal reaction to James's overtures seemed to have been justified. An explanation for her hesitance may have been provided by Edmund Tremayne, one of the Privy Council clerks who was also in Walsingham's employ. He was keeping his master in touch with affairs at Court in an informal and personal way. He had talked with Vice-Chamberlain Hatton, whose service Walsingham had arranged for him to join temporarily. The Queen had apparently told Hatton that 'it was against her heart to entertain them [the Scottish envoys] as ambassadors'. Tremayne implied that Elizabeth could not bring herself formally to accept James as king in the lifetime of Mary Queen of Scots and thus acknowledge that crowned heads could be toppled.

All was not to be lost, however, and a few days later Elizabeth seemed to be going to have it both ways. Having made her gesture and salved her conscience, she indicated that she would be willing to provide help for James if necessary. Wilson reported to Walsingham in rather guarded terms that 'hope is given that the King shall not want aid hereafter'. Some inkling of this change of heart may have caught up with Dunfermline on his way home. When he reached Edinburgh and had 'exponit and declarit the form of his proceidings and negotiatioun with the Quenis

43

Queen Elizabeth receiving two foreign emissaries, 1580s (detail, artist unknown). These were Dutch but the scene at Melford would have been very similar. The two foreigners are accompanied by their ambassador. The floor is covered in matting and the Queen's chair has a canopy like the 'throne' at Kimberley.

Majestie of England and hir Counsale', the Privy Council of Scotland declared him to have 'trewlie, honestlie and diligentlie performit and dischairgit his charge'.[11]

About ten days later Bernardino de Mendoza, the Spanish ambassador in London, reported to Madrid an incident which must have taken place at Melford Hall. He had arrived in England only a few months earlier but he was able to follow Elizabeth's dealings with the French very closely through his informants with the progress. One of these had said that on an occasion when de Bacqueville was dining with the Queen, she decided that the gold and silver plate on the sideboard was not as impressive as she would have liked the French to see. This was, of course, her own plate, brought by John Pigion from the Jewel House, so she sent for the Lord Chamberlain and asked him why there was so little. Lord Sussex replied that he had accompanied a great many progresses and had never known so much plate to be carried as on this one. The Queen told him to hold his tongue and abused him vigorously. Then she turned to Lord North and asked his opinion. North was no friend of Sussex and predictably he agreed with the Queen. The quarrel between Sussex and North continued outside the royal presence, Sussex eventually trying, vainly, to gain Leicester's support.[12]

Mendoza's story is borne out by an apparent sequel. In spite of his protestations, the Lord Chamberlain evidently took the Queen's censures to heart, for he sent Pigion back to London to collect more plate for the next two major stops. By using six horses to cover the ground quickly, he was able to return with 'certayne riche Cuppes, standing Trenchers and Salte of golde and other thinges' in time for Elizabeth to use them at Kenninghall Palace and in Norwich.

The following day, again according to Mendoza, Elizabeth wanted the Earl of Oxford, who was travelling with the progress, to dance for the French party. Twice, however, he refused and would not listen to her messenger, saying he did not wish to entertain Frenchmen. The Earl, Edward de Vere, then aged twenty-eight, was a feckless and eccentric courtier who often fell foul of the Queen but usually managed to return to favour. Mendoza was interested because he had heard that Oxford had expressed a wish to go and serve his master, the King of Spain. (Indeed, for a time later in his life Oxford was converted to Catholicism.) In 1571 Oxford had married Burghley's beloved elder daughter, Anne, then only fifteen; the Queen had attended their wedding. The marriage was very quickly in trouble, Oxford alleging that their first child was not his. He remained estranged for several years, causing Anne much unhappiness. They were reconciled only in 1582, six years before her death at the age of thirty-two. His relations with her father can never have been cordial, though Burghley tried to help him from time to time for Anne's sake.

Among all the entertainments government business had to continue. The eight regular members of the Council met twice at Melford, dealing with the usual crop of less important concerns alongside their continuing preoccupation with foreign affairs.

Edward de Vere, 17th Earl of Oxford, irresponsible courtier and husband of Anne Cecil, daughter of Lord Burghley (artist unknown, private collection).

On 3 August they instructed the Lord Mayor of London to exempt the Warden of Her Majesty's Mint from all other appointments; the next day they ordered an inquiry into the disappearance of certain goods from a Danish ship on the Welsh coast and the auditing of the books of the recently dead Keeper of the Ordnance. They also authorized the payment of two municipal officers from Dover who had brought up a prisoner, for the cost of their horses, their food and their guide.

Again messengers arrived from and left for the Low Countries. Another had already been to Ireland, where he had waited a week for replies to the letters he carried and a ship to Liverpool, and returned to Greenwich. He had then followed the Council to Melford and was about to set off again via London to York and Berwick.

Other officials visited or stayed in Sudbury nearby. The Town Book records several payments to them: $10d$ for the Harbingers' wine and beer, $12s\,4d$ to 'the Clarke of the markettes of the Queen's house and others at the Crowne', and a total of $41s\,4d$ to other minor officials. Sir William Cordell's brother (probably Edward, who later became a Suffolk JP) received $12d$ and there was $4s\,8d$ for wine given to Lord Chamberlain Sussex.[13]

To Bury St Edmunds

The Queen left Melford Hall early in the morning on 5 August and dined at Lawshall Hall, the home of Henry Drury, a local landowner, 'to the great rejoycing of the said parish and the country thereabouts' as recorded in the parish register.[14] Henry was a Catholic and was soon to suffer for his adherence to the old faith. For the moment, however, all seems to have gone smoothly while the Queen was at his house. The preparations at Lawshall were made by Richard Conysbie, 'Extraordinary' Gentleman Usher (that is, he was not on the regular staff), who must have been in attendance on other duties and now assembled a nine-man team to provide some temporary help for the two regular ushers. At all events, he was not used again until the progress was well on the way back. Charles Smythe, moving on from Kedington, came as usual for one day.

In the evening Elizabeth rode the 4 miles on to Bury St Edmunds, where Anthony Wingfeld, coming from Kedington and Cavendish, spent the usual six days. Charles Smythe rode straight on from Lawshall to stay four. Elizabeth was to spend four nights there, lodged in 'the old Abby', in a house created from the monastic buildings which then belonged to Thomas Badby,[15] a rich and active local Puritan. A month earlier he had donated Shire House and some of the former abbey land for use by the Justices and the Courts.[16] He was the uncle of Robert Jermyn of Rushbrooke (soon to be knighted) and when he died in 1583 he was buried in Rushbrooke Church. His house was not big enough even for the Queen's most senior ministers and both Lord Burghley and Lord Leicester stayed with Thomas Andrews in a house outside the abbey.[17] He was another wealthy Bury citizen, frequently opposing Badby's Puritan views.[18] He was born in Bury and when he died in 1585 he was buried, as he wished, with his forebears in the churchyard of St James's, now the cathedral.[19]

The next day, Wednesday 6 August, the Privy Council met in Bury St Edmunds. Two of the regular members were absent, Lord Leicester (though he was still in Bury) and his brother Lord Warwick. The other six dealt with some minor matters. They received the persistent Secretary of the Steelyard, the trading centre of the Hanseatic merchants, and repeated what they had said to him at Havering about the Queen's support for the export of white cloth; and, at the request of the French ambassador, who was, of course, in Bury, they instructed the London authorities to release a Frenchman from the Fleet prison (he was to be told that none of Her Majesty's own subjects would have been so favoured).

That evening John North rejoined the progress from Kirtling. Not being a member of the Court, he had to find his own accommodation and he took a room for the night, paying 12d. He had only two servants of his own and relied for help during these incursions into the complex world of a progress on some of Lord Leicester's men, who had to be rewarded with 12d or 18d. He went home again the next day, Thursday, when the Queen might also have been expected to leave.[20]

At about the same time the Queen's presence in the town was recorded without comment in St James's parish register.[21] By 8 August Lord Burghley had learned enough of the people of the town to comment on their attitude to religion. He wrote that he had found them 'very sound saving in some part affected with the brainsick heresy of the papistical Family of Love'. The Family of Love was a heretical sect, much feared in England, which gained such strength in the east of the country that in 1580 a proclamation was issued against it. All its adherents, who believed that only they would be saved on Judgement Day and all others rejected and damned, were to be sought out and punished and the printers and possessors of their books were to be imprisoned. Most of the citizens, however, saw nothing to fear in the Council's presence; a week later the Puritan parishioners of St James sought Burghley's support for their preacher, whose teaching had been criticized.[22]

The progress halted in Bury St Edmunds longer than usual and everyone, including the Queen, used the comparative peace to write copiously. Well over a dozen letters were sent abroad.

On 7 August Lord Leicester, writing to Walsingham, described another difficulty met by the Council in dealing with the Queen. She had been reluctant to deal with any but the most urgent state business: 'Our conference with Her Majesty about affairs, more than by necessity is urged, is both seldom and slender.' She had had a cold and frequent recurrences of the pain in her face, perhaps from the tooth which had troubled her in May, but now, feeling better, 'was perhaps the more loth to trouble herself' with work. Leicester ended his letter, 'In much haste, Her Majesty ready to horseback'.

Leicester had already told Walsingham that the Queen was 'much offended' with him. On the following day Lord Burghley also wrote to Walsingham, giving him the background to a letter he would receive from the Queen. She had dictated it in haste and then, to Burghley's relief, had apparently lost interest in it. In the middle of the next afternoon, however, she had suddenly demanded to know why it had not been dispatched. Burghley replied 'merrily' that 'without signing it could neither go nor ride'. Eventually, in spite of reservations felt by Burghley, Lord Leicester and Secretary Wilson, she listened to de Bacqueville and Mauvissière and signed the letter. Perhaps because the Frenchmen knew about this letter, Monsieur de Quissé was sent off to the Low Countries, apparently to see both his master Alençon and also Walsingham, to whom he carried a letter from Secretary Wilson; it commented that he, de Quissé, 'is well accounted of by Hir Majesty'.

It is not surprising that the Queen's letter to Walsingham had caused Lord Burghley some anxiety. In it Elizabeth chided him for failing to carry out her instructions to contact the Duc d'Alençon now in the Netherlands. The Queen had begun to fear that all his envoys' fine phrases about his wanting to marry her and promises that he would take no step without her agreement might be a blind to distract attention from a French takeover. Walsingham must 'press him to know his intentions'. She was also disturbed by her ambassadors' failure to bring about a peaceful settlement. Nevertheless, she was aware 'of both your good wills and faithful meaning' and they should not be grieved by her complaints – though there was a sting in the tail of the letter: 'You, Walsingham, shall at your return know what we have misliked in your actions.' The veiled threat was probably not greatly lessened by her adding that she would be willing 'like a good mistress' to hear his explanations 'with our accustomed favour'.

The Queen's apparent displeasure led colleagues to write to Walsingham reassuringly. Her final words, wrote Burghley, were said 'with no anger at all'. Mr Secretary Wilson also wrote 'touching Her Majesty's judgement of your service'. He did not know of 'any such misliking conceived as you are informed'. All Walsingham's efforts, other than his failure to see Alençon, had been 'taken in very good part'.

Faced with such conflicting evidence from home, the English ambassadors in the Netherlands were becoming disillusioned about their mission and alarmed about their personal position. Already a week earlier, Walsingham expected 'a hard welcome' on his return and was threatening to retire from active politics.

Another letter from Burghley the next day, 9 August, illustrated yet again the difficulty of conducting foreign affairs while on progress with an unpredictable Queen. Walsingham would have received a second letter from Elizabeth conceding that if there were any real danger of Alençon's seeking power for himself in the Netherlands or going over to the Spanish side, he could offer the Dutch help in men and money – but circumspectly. Burghley explained that she had consulted only himself, Lord Leicester and Sir Christopher Hatton before deciding on this step and Burghley had had to write the letter as she dictated it, 'in haste while she was making ready to horse'. He had had no time to make a clean copy. His letter was carried by a courier who had arrived in Bury St Edmunds only on 6 August.

Some of the Council's letters written at Bury were dispatched from Thetford, about 12 miles away, where some officials were installed. Indeed, on two occasions Secretary Wilson himself signed letters from Thetford. As well as the movements of Court officers between local bases, there was the usual coming and going of messengers. Among them was a gentleman of Lord Cobham's staff who had reached the Court at Audley End and had ridden on to Bury with them. He was authorized by the Council to hire horses and ships to return via Harwich with some of the mail, including the Queen's first letter. A courier from Walsingham who reached Bury later was similarly authorized to return. He collected the Queen's second letter from the clerks at Thetford and finally left from Euston, where Wilson was already installed ahead of the Queen's arrival.

Several Suffolk gentlemen with acceptable religious credentials were knighted by the Queen while she was in Bury. Churchyard listed their names. Robert Jermyn of Rushbrooke, another very wealthy local landowner, and Sheriff William Spring of Pakenham were both good Protestants who, according to Churchyard, kept open house while the progress was in the vicinity, Jermyn twice feasting the French ambassadors 'with whiche charges and courtesie they stood marvellously contented'. They probably also provided accommodation for many of the entourage. Thomas Kytson of Hengrave, a conformist to the Protestant faith, was equally hospitable and was to entertain the Queen herself on her return journey. Arthur Heveningham had estates in the east of Suffolk and in Ketteringham, south of Norwich, and was a leading figure in both counties for many years. The sixth man on Churchyard's list was Philip Parker, a magistrate who was prominent in Suffolk affairs.

During her stay in Bury the Queen visited the recently rebuilt manor house of Sir William Drury (nephew of Henry but not of his Catholic persuasion) at Hawstead, where, according to local tradition, she dropped a silver-handled fan into the moat. Over 200 years later there remained in the courtyard facing the main gateway a stone fountain dated 1578, evidently put up for this occasion. In the centre of the basin stood a statue of Hercules filling it with water in a rather indecorous manner.[23] At Hawstead, said Churchyard, the Queen was given 'a costly and delicat dinner'. Anthony Wingfeld spent two days setting up 'a dyninge chamber' there and Charles Smythe came for one day, in addition to their time in Bury. An earlier Drury had been allowed to enclose 2,000 acres for a deer park, so Elizabeth was able to go hunting there.

The Hercules statue at Hawstead Hall, Suffolk (artist's impression based on an engraving in Cullum's *History of Hawstead*, 1813).

Sir William Drury was well known to the Queen. He had married Elizabeth Stafford, one of the Ladies of the Bedchamber, who had had a baby early in the year but by now was probably back on duty and travelling with the progress. The Queen's New Year gifts in 1579 included from Sir William 'a paire of myttows [mittens] of blake vellet enbraudered with damaske gold and lyned with unshorne vellet carnation'. Lady Drury's gift was 'a foreparte of clothe of silver all over enbraudred with clothe of gold'. Both received the usual pieces of silver gilt in return, including ten spoons. Sir William's name appeared in the list on several subsequent occasions.

In 1589, then a colonel in France, he quarrelled with another colonel over precedence and was killed in the ensuing duel. His body was brought back to England and buried in the chancel of Hawstead Church, where a marble bust and memorial still survive. The Queen wrote to comfort his widow, calling her 'my Bess' and reminding her that she still had a queen 'who leves not now to protecte you when your case requires care and minds not to omitte whatever may be best for you and yours'.[24] Sir William was succeeded by his son Robert, a friend of the poet John Donne. When Robert's only surviving child, Elizabeth, died in 1610 aged fourteen, it was almost certainly Donne who composed the Latin epitaph on her delicately decorated tomb in Hawstead Church, and he later wrote two long elegies to her. The first, written on the anniversary of her death, so moved her father that Donne and his family were given rent-free accommodation in his London house in Drury Lane.[25] Another briefer and perhaps more moving epitaph in the church records the earlier death of another daughter, Dorothy, aged four:

> She promised much
> Too soon untied
> She only dreamt she lived
> And then she dyed

Another of the Queen's ladies was honoured while the progress was at Bury St Edmunds. This was the Swedish Helena Snakenburg, who, some thirteen years earlier, had come to England as a young girl in the entourage of Princess Cecilia, an admirer of Queen Elizabeth. Within a few days of her arrival in England the princess had given birth to a baby whose christening a fortnight later in the chapel of Whitehall Palace was attended by Elizabeth. Among her gentlemen was William Parr, brother of Henry VIII's last queen, now the Marquess of Northampton, aged fifty-two. His second wife, whom he had married in rather dubious circumstances, had recently died and he and young Helena were immediately attracted to one another. By the spring of the following year Helena had agreed to marry William and refused to return home when the princess left. She was able to stay because the Queen had taken a liking to her and made her a Gentlewoman of the Privy Chamber. In April 1571, when Helena

Helena Snakenburg, Marchioness of Northampton, between her two husbands, William Parr and Thomas Gorges (detail from a genealogical tree, British Library, Lansdowne Roll 9).

was twenty-one, she and William married; the Queen attended their wedding. Sadly, by the end of the year William was dead.

His widow stayed on in England and some years later she married again, incurring, as her ladies often did, the Queen's displeasure. By June 1578, however, she had returned to favour and the birth of her daughter, christened Elizabeth, was marked by the Queen with the gift of a silver-gilt bowl.[26] It was delivered to Helena on 7 August, though it is not clear whether she was by then in attendance on the Queen or at home in Middlesex. Her gift to the Queen the following New Year was a gold girdle with gold buckles and pendants decorated with 'sparcks' of rubies and diamonds, as well as ten pearls set in gold. Like other widows of eminent men, she retained her first husband's title, so her gift was listed as from the Lady Marquess of Northampton.

On 8 August the parish clerk of St James's Church recorded the first of a number of deaths from plague. Of the twenty-five deaths in the parish register for the rest of the year, twenty-three were from plague and they continued in 1579.[27] It is all too possible the progress brought it with them. (Norwich also suffered a serious outbreak after they left.)

To Kenninghall

Elizabeth probably left Bury St Edmunds after dinner on Saturday 9 August, arriving at Mr Rookwood's house at Euston, about 10 miles to the north, in the afternoon. Symon Bowyer and his team had come on from Melford Hall for the usual six days and Raphe Hope, on his return from Westminster, stayed three. The Queen stayed two nights.

Some Council officials, including Secretary Wilson, were already working there. A courier arrived from Paris on the Monday when they were already moving on and could not be paid until they reached Kenninghall.

The Queen's host, Edward Rookwood of Euston, was a young man belonging to a Suffolk family of Catholics. (Another Rookwood, Ambrose, who lived at Coldham Hall, Stanningfield, south of Bury, was executed after the Gunpowder Plot.) Euston was conveniently about half-way between Bury and Kenninghall, the Queen's next lodging, but Rookwood's religion could not have escaped notice when her itinerary was being drawn up and what followed may have been engineered as a demonstration of the Council's intentions.

Unfortunately, the only detailed account of events on the Sunday was given three weeks later by the same Richard Topclyffe who recorded the Queen's pleasure at Leicester's return to Court. As he was an extreme anti-Catholic, his description of the incident at Euston was by no means unbiased. At first, apparently, things went pleasantly enough and Rookwood was brought into the Queen's presence. Unaware of what was to follow, she gave him her hand to kiss and thanked him for the use of his house. Then, however, Lord Chamberlain Sussex, who knew that Rookwood had been excommunicated for his Catholicism, summoned him, berated him for daring to come before the Queen and ordered him to leave the Court – in effect to get out of his own house.

To make matters worse, a piece of the plate which had been brought by the royal servants for use by the Court was lost. During the search for it, the most telling evidence against Rookwood, a statue of Our Lady, was found hidden in a hayrick and carried into the Queen's presence while she was watching some country dancing. Amid general consternation, she commanded that it be burnt and watched while her order was promptly carried out by the local people, 'to her content', said Topclyffe, 'and unspeakable joy of every one but some one or two who had sucked of the idoll's poysoned mylke'.[28]

A different account of what was probably the same incident was reported by the Spanish ambassador in London. He was writing on 14 August, so his informant must have set out as soon as the Queen left Euston. He had learned that there were many Catholics 'in the North where the Queen is travelling' – apparently Mendoza's knowledge of English geography was not yet very reliable. At one of the houses where she had stayed, 'her people found an altar with all the ornaments thereupon ready for the celebration of Mass'; improbably, 'the gentleman, his wife and children received the Queen with crucifixes round their necks'.[29]

Within a few days Rookwood was summoned to appear before the Council sitting with the Bishop in Norwich, to be questioned about his recusancy. He was evidently regarded as a special case, for other Suffolk gentlemen were examined in their own county without the bishop's presence.

On the Sunday of all this excitement, John North again caught up with the progress. This time he was to stay with it for nearly a fortnight. He left home in the afternoon and was able to find somewhere to spend that night at Euston, although accommodation there was limited and many people were lodged elsewhere.[30]

Lord Leicester stayed in a house belonging to a Mr Methwold at 'Rushworth' – now Rushford – about 3 miles from Euston, and his men went to Thetford,[31] where some people were already based. The manor of Rushworth had belonged to an ecclesiastical college founded in the fourteenth century by Edmund de Gonville, who later founded the Cambridge college named after him. After the Dissolution of the Monasteries, it came into the possession of the 3rd Duke of Norfolk but reverted to the Crown when he was imprisoned for treason in 1547. The young Edward VI granted the manor to his tutor Sir John Cheke, who conveyed it to Sir George Alington, who had married Sir John's sister. Their daughter married William Methwold, who evidently took over the lease when Sir John died in 1557.[32] She would have been able to report on the invasion by Court officials to her uncle Sir Giles Alington, with whom the Queen was to stay on her way home.

A pair of gloves preserved at Hatfield House is traditionally said to have been left by Elizabeth at Shadwell Lodge near Rushford on her way to Norwich. This house was not built until the eighteenth century but it was owned by a descendant of Robert Buxton, to whom Methwold transferred the lease of the college lands in 1585, so it is possible that they were indeed left at Rushford as a consequence of Lord Leicester's staying here.

On Monday 11 August the Queen left Euston after dinner and crossed into Norfolk en route for Kenninghall Palace. The splendour of her procession continued. She was met at the county boundary by the Sheriff of Norfolk, accompanied, according to Churchyard, by 2,500 horsemen, including 600 gentlemen 'bravely attired and mounted'. 'The Norfolk gentlemen', he said, 'hearing how dutifullie their neybours had receyved the Prince prepared in lyke sort to shewe themselves dutifull and so in most gallantest manner assembled and set forward . . . . the bankets and feastes began heere afresh.'

Among the Norfolk gentlemen was Sir Nicholas Lestrange, a JP from north-west Norfolk, who had started out from King's Lynn the previous day with six men and twelve horses. He followed the progress to Norwich (where he took the opportunity to do a little private legal business) and back to Thetford. At Kenninghall Lestrange was lodged in a tent and his men and horses were dispersed to Larling and to West Harling, where his steward's father lived.[33] Many other gentlemen will have done much the same in Norfolk as in the other counties she crossed, joining and considerably inflating the Queen's train and the problems of provisioning and housing along the way. Nevertheless, Churchyard's figures for the size of the parties welcoming the Queen into both Norfolk and Suffolk were probably overestimates; a

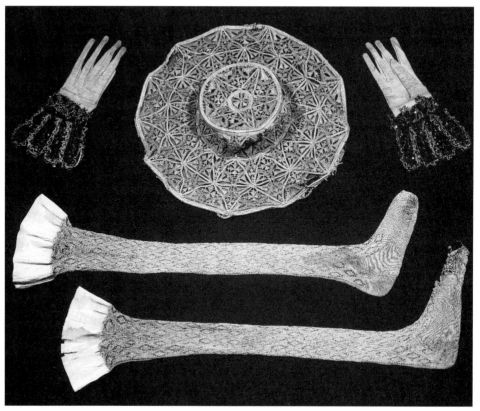

The gloves said to have been left by Queen Elizabeth on her way to Norwich (the hat and stockings are also traditionally associated with her).

list of all the gentlemen in Norfolk which was prepared for Lord Burghley totalled only 324 names.

By that Monday evening the progress had arrived at the great palace begun by the 2nd Duke of Norfolk and first occupied by his son as 3rd Duke in 1526. In 1578 it belonged to Philip, Earl of Surrey, whose title had been restored after the execution for high treason of his father, the 4th Duke, just over six years earlier. Thomas Howard, the 4th Duke, though nominally a Protestant all his life, had married as his third wife the Catholic Elizabeth Dacre and a year after her death had planned to marry Mary Queen of Scots. Having failed in this, he later became involved in the plot to remove Elizabeth and put Mary on the throne which led to his execution.

In the course of the sixteenth century the Dukes of Norfolk had become very rich. When the 4th Duke (the last to live in Norfolk) was imprisoned for treason in 1571, the Council instructed four eminent local men to make an inventory of his possessions in Norfolk. The contents of Kenninghall Palace were listed room by room, from the Great Chamber and the Dining Chamber through the rooms of members of the family and their senior servants, such as the steward and the master of horse – they usually had two rooms each, an inner and an outer chamber – to those of the stable grooms and the gardener, about forty in all. The schoolmaster had his own quarters and there was a nursery – five of the Duke's children and stepchildren were still under eleven.

Although the investigators reported that the Duke had apparently taken to London and sold much of his silver and jewels, there was still plenty of evidence of the richness of the furnishings and the wealth of the family. The Great Chamber contained seven tapestries depicting the history of Hercules and two Turkey carpets. The Earl of Surrey's chamber – he was fourteen at the time – had a walnut bedstead with a canopy of purple velvet, a double valence and curtains of fine purple silk and a chair with a purple velvet cushion. Lady Surrey's bed (Anne was a little older than Philip) also had a purple canopy and valence decorated with gold lace and fringed with purple and gold; her curtains were of blue silk and her chair was covered in crimson velvet fringed with red silk and silver. Even the gardener's chamber contained a bedstead, a featherbed and bolster, a pair of sheets and a bedcover.

The inventory also listed the clothes of the last Duchess, Elizabeth, who had died in childbirth in 1567, four years before her husband's execution. Over forty items were in the charge of the Yeoman of the Robes, including three straight-backed gowns, eleven loose gowns (probably worn by pregnant ladies), eleven foreparts, four French kirtles and five pairs of French sleeves, mostly in velvet or satin and embroidered with gold and silver. There were also 'Twoe cradle cloths of crimson satin quilted'. The Duke's garments were mostly listed as 'broken' and had perhaps been abandoned at Kenninghall.[34]

When the inventory had been taken the palace was closed down and, as we have seen, the Duke's children were sent to Audley End, escorted by Sir Nicholas Lestrange, then one of the staff. It was probably not used again until it was opened up for the Queen's visit some seven years later and William Bowles arrived on his tour of inspection. Some of the contents may well have still been in place and the Great Chamber and the Dining Chamber would have been prepared for her use with additional Howard hangings and furnishings as Anthony Wingfeld and his men thought fit when they arrived from Bury St Edmunds and Hawstead to spend seven days at Kenninghall. They also made 'a standinge house thereby' from which the Queen and her party could shoot the deer with crossbows as they were driven past. Raphe Hope came for three days and John Pigion arrived back from London with the extra plate. Sir Nicholas, remembering the

The Queen and her ladies on a 'standing' in a forest: the huntsman has located a deer and brings its droppings ('fewmets') on a bed of leaves to show what a fine beast it is (Turbervile's *Booke of Hunting*, 1576).

splendid lifestyle under the Duke, must have seen the great house opened up again with mixed feelings.

Philip Howard, Earl of Surrey, the Queen's host, was the son of the 4th Duke's first wife, Mary Fitzalan of Arundel, through whom he acquired the title Earl of Arundel and the castle. A year before his father's death, while they were still children, he had married Anne (familiarly known as Nanne), the daughter of his Catholic stepmother, and in years to come he was to suffer for his conversion to their faith. Like his father, grandfather and great-grandfather (who escaped execution only by the death of Henry VIII), he was to be imprisoned in the Tower and condemned to death. Eventually his sentence was commuted and he died in the Tower some years later in 1595. While he was in prison, his house in London, Arundel House in the Strand, was used by Anne as a refuge for Catholic priests.

In 1578, however, Philip's encounters with the Queen on her progress passed off without harm to him, except that entertaining her at Kenninghall and again at Surrey House in Norwich cost him £10,000 and left him deeply in debt. (He may well have been with the progress all along; he was present when the Queen stayed at his half-brother's house at Audley End, as we have seen.) At Kenninghall, according to Churchyard, 'The Earle of Surrey did shewe most sumptuous cheere in whose parke were speeches well sette out and a speciall device much comended'; he also presented the Queen with a jewel.[35] The following New Year Surrey incurred even further expense, giving her 'a gyrdill of tawny vellet embrawdred wth sede perle, the buckle and pendant of golde'.

The Council met twice while they were at Kenninghall. On 11 August, soon after they got there, they heard that the Sheriff of Pembrokeshire had arrived in obedience to their summons issued at Standon. He had evidently made considerable haste, for he was well within the fourteen days allowed him. Nevertheless, he had to wait until the Council met in Norwich for his hearing. The next day there was further evidence of the Queen's support for young James of Scotland when they ordered her troops in the north to be ready, not only to defend the English border but also to offer help to the King if necessary against 'any his disobedient servants'.

Business on that day also included authorizing the payment of the Court Post Master, Thomas Randolph, in accordance with their order of 13 July. In fact, it was his deputy, Robert Gascoigne, who was paid four days later when the Court reached Norwich, for 'such postes as have been and are to be laide in sundrie places for the service of Her Majestie during the tyme of Her Majestie's Progresse'. The post from London to Kenninghall, carried by courier and a series of post horses, normally came via Newmarket and Thetford and took three to seven days. As usual, couriers came and went. One left Kenninghall for Paris and on 14 August Nicholas Fante, who had been educated at Norwich Grammar School,[36] returned to his native county, arriving from Flanders just as everyone was leaving.

Philip Howard, Earl of Surrey, son and heir of the 4th Duke of Norfolk, owner of Kenninghall Palace and Surrey House in Norwich (attributed to George Gower).

To Norwich

Elizabeth spent three nights at Kenninghall and then on Thursday 14 August she moved on to Bracon Ash, about 5 miles south of Norwich. Again there is no record of a stop for dinner, though she had a 12 mile ride. It was probably somewhere on the way, perhaps during a picnic stop, that she was presented with a gift from the little town of Pulham St Mary Magdalen; they later recorded the payment of £11 for 'a platte of gould for to gyve oure Sovryne Ladye the Quene'.[37] Pulham is rather south of the direct route from Kenninghall to Bracon Ash, so perhaps a deputation intercepted the procession along the way. They probably knew that William Bowles had called at the house of Mr (soon to be Sir) Thomas Gaudy at Redenhall, only 3 miles away, and so expected the progress to pass near or even through Pulham on its way to Norwich.

At Bracon Ash the Queen stayed at 'Mr Townesendes', where Symon Bowyer, coming from Euston, spent six days and Charles Smythe three. Thomas Townsend, a member of an important Norfolk family, the Townsends of Raynham, had bought the manor of Bracon Ash some years earlier. He had married Elizabeth, Lady Stile, widow of Sir Humphrey Stile of Beckenham in Kent, another lady who continued to use her earlier superior title. Both inclined to the old religion and some years earlier, following an order of 1571 to root out the recusants in his diocese, Bishop Parkhurst of Norwich had chided them for not attending church. Thomas was apparently showing signs of conforming, but 'touching my lady I hear she is wilfully bent' and there was evidently little hope of her reformation. Both were warned that henceforth they were to come to church and receive the sacrament 'as becometh Christians', or the bishop would report them to the Council.[38] They would then become liable for the heavy fine of 12d for every failure to attend church on Sundays and Holy Days which could soon mount up to a crippling sum. Nevertheless, Thomas seems to have remained recalcitrant and in 1576 he was indeed reported to the Council for recusancy. However, by then a new bishop, Freake, was in office and, as the Council suspected, he was less fervently reforming than his predecessor and no harm came to Thomas. Lady Stile too seems to have continued to go the old way in religion and after her death in 1580 she was still listed as a recusant.

Unlike some others whose houses were used by the Queen on her progress, both survived her visit without suffering more than the usual inconvenience and expense.

Their house was Mergate Hall, which had been built by a John Appleyard in the fifteenth century and had come down to another John Appleyard who had been High Sheriff of Norfolk and Suffolk in 1559. This Appleyard's father had married Elizabeth Robsart, mother of Amy, the ill-fated wife of Robert Dudley, now Lord Leicester. The young couple probably met when Robert, aged seventeen, came to Norfolk with his father, the Earl of Warwick (later Duke of Northumberland), to put down Kett's Rebellion in 1549. Certainly they were married in the following year and for some time they lived in Norfolk, where the young Robert obtained a number of important posts.

Now, over a quarter of a century later, while the Queen stayed at Mergate Hall, Lord Leicester was lodged at 'Mr Flowerduies'.[39] This was Stanfield Hall, about 2 miles away, which had also belonged to John Appleyard, who had acquired it through his marriage to Elizabeth Robsart. Leicester knew it well – he and his father had stayed there in 1549. Now it belonged to Edward Flowerdew, an eminent local lawyer who later rose to positions of national importance. His brother, William, had married Amy's half-sister Frances Appleyard.[40]

With Leicester's return there, many local people must have remembered his marriage to a local heiress and her sudden, unexplained death ten years later, when she was found with a broken neck at the foot of the stairs in her house, Cumnor Place, in Berkshire. At the request of Leicester, who did not go himself, her grand funeral in Oxford was attended by her half-brother, the John Appleyard who had owned the house where the Queen was now staying.[41] It was said that her absent husband had arranged her death in order to be free to marry the Queen. Nothing was proved and in the eighteen years since she died he had not married Elizabeth or anyone else. Ironically, he was now planning a second, secret, marriage.

Unaware, the Queen moved on towards Norwich, the culmination and turning point of her long journey. On the morning of 16 August the vast train assembled once more for the last lap. The Queen left Bracon Ash after the late morning meal to ride the last few miles. Somewhere along the 5 mile route Anthony Wingfeld had taken over a house where she could change into more gorgeous clothes, and prepare herself for the reception awaiting her at the city boundary. Already a great crowd of dignitaries, their servants, officials and the common people were gathering to greet her.

CHAPTER 4

NORWICH

16–22 AUGUST

The City's Preparations

In 1578 Norwich was the second city of the kingdom, with a population of just over 16,000 (London's was around 200,000). It was governed by an Assembly, consisting of the Mayor, two Sheriffs, twenty-four aldermen and sixty commoners. The whole group met only four times a year unless specially summoned, but the Mayor and aldermen met twice a week to deal with the routine running of the city.

The worsted weaving trade which had brought Norwich prosperity had seriously declined by the middle of the sixteenth century and in 1565 a limited number of foreign master workmen with their families had been granted permission to move there to supplement and diversify the local industry. Others followed and in spite of the restrictions placed on them and sporadic outbreaks of local opposition, towards the end of the 1570s foreign workers and their families totalled about 6,000. They were largely Protestant refugees from Spanish Catholicism in the Low Countries, mainly 'Dutchmen' from Flanders and a smaller number of French-speaking Walloons.[1]

The city had been warned of the Queen's impending visit by the middle of June and from the 20th to the end of the month, the Mayor issued a series of orders about the preparations to be made. These exceptional measures, which were put into effect for a comparatively short period, present a quite alarming picture of conditions in the city in normal times. The exact date of the Queen's arrival and the details of her route and programme were evidently not known. A margin of time was allowed for the work to be done and the parts of the city given particular attention do not exactly match her known movements there. Perhaps – though it seems unlikely – there was nothing to do elsewhere.

Major works were undertaken to clean up and tidy the city, particularly the approaches through the gates and over the River Wensum. The roadway outside St

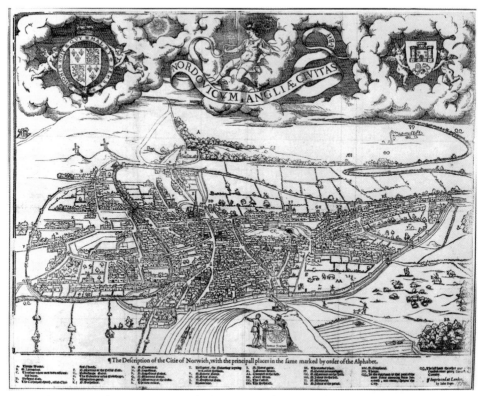

Cunningham's map of Norwich, 1558. The Queen entered the city through St Stephen's Gate (on the right), passed through the market and on to the cathedral. She left through St Giles's Gate (bottom centre). Surrey House, then still called St Leonard's Priory, is across the river above the Cathedral.

Stephen's Gate was to be gravelled and that outside St Giles's Gate was to be widened, levelled and also gravelled; the muckhill at Brazen Gates was to be 'cleane taken away' (but only to 'some other grounde nere adioyning'); and White Friars Bridge was to be repaired with 'planke and borde'. More drastically, the wall of St John's churchyard was to be taken down to widen the street and rebuilt; the parish would be allowed £5 towards the cost. (This was either St John's Sepulchre Church, just inside Ber Street Gate or St John's Maddermarket, which in the event proved to be on the Queen's route to St Benet's Gate and Costessey.) In the city centre the market cross was to be repainted, 'tymber color' and white, and the pillory and cage were to be removed three or four days before she arrived – miscreants were not to escape, however; another pillory would have to be made to serve for the time being. Help would be needed to get all this work done in time and messengers were sent to the mayors of King's Lynn and elsewhere, asking them to send in skilled masons; reasonable travelling expenses would be paid.

The citizens also had their orders. By the end of July the outsides of their houses had to be cleaned and plastered, though only 'towards the stretes side'; they too could call in craftsmen – masons, carpenters, joiners, reeders (thatchers), tilers, plasterers and painters – to work with them on 'the reparing and bewtefying' of their houses; the ban on workmen from outside the city which usually protected its own tradesmen was lifted until the end of August. Householders had to repair the pathways outside their houses or at least fill in the worst holes with gravel, and their 'necessaries' (privies) on the riverbank had to be cleaned up by 6 August. Anyone who had no convenient privy had to make suitable arrangements – the lanes and streets were not to be polluted. Finally, all the chimneys had to be swept and anyone whose chimney caught fire would be fined $6s\ 8d$. Indeed, failure to observe any of these orders was punishable by a fine.

There were other instructions intended to keep the city wholesome during the visit. Until the end of August all butchers who killed their beasts within the city were to take away the waste and bury it somewhere outside. No cows were to be brought into the city to be milked; they were to be milked either in the fields or 'at home in ther yarde'. For the whole of August it was forbidden to keep any horse, cow or pig in the castle ditches or in the town ditches or lanes. And nobody preparing wool for spinning was to empty the water or throw the waste into the street.

The Assembly considered what extra provisions would be needed when the several hundred people accompanying the Queen moved into the city. Again they lifted their normal restrictions on tradesmen from outside. During the Queen's visit butchers and food merchants would be allowed to bring in and sell their products in the open market, provided it was 'good and helthesome for mans body'.

There would also be a need for extra transport. Many more post horses would be needed and every innkeeper was to keep 'one good and able horse' ready for use when required. Failure would mean a significant fine of $20s$. On the river, three boats were to be converted to barges for the Court's use and as many other boats as possible were to be equipped with awnings.

Towards the end of July the question of entertainments was considered. The Waits or town musicians were to be paid their annual wages in advance, $26s\ 8d$, and given in addition $13s\ 4d$ towards their uniforms. There would also be the cost of the 'shows' to be put on (the impresario Churchyard had already arrived in Norwich by then) and there would be presents to be given to members of the Council and officers and servants of the Queen. It was decided to borrow £400 or £500 for the purpose.[2]

Later the Court officials began their routine preparations. Gentleman Usher Anthony Wingfeld and his nine men arrived from Kenninghall and spent at least six days in Norwich. Raphe Hope and his two men spent four days working on 'the Office of Her Majesty's Roabes'.

Earlier, as we have seen, Thomas Churchyard had been sent on ahead by the Vice-Chamberlain to organize some of the 'shows'. Others, Bernard Garter and Henry Goldingham, had followed. Churchyard and Garter each wrote an account of his work, dedicated to a patron in London and published remarkably soon after the events described; Garter's was registered at the Company of Stationers on 30 August and Churchyard's on 20 September. Between them they provided a detailed day-to-day account of many of the Queen's social engagements. Churchyard's introduction claimed that what he wrote was true because he saw it or heard it credibly described. He had arrived in Norwich three weeks ahead of the progress, 'employed to sette forth some shewes' and had spent the time 'devising and studying the best I coulde for the Citie'. His account included details of the performances which the Queen saw 'and gave gratious thankes for', as well as those which she did not see 'by meanes of evill weather'. Goldingham and Garter 'dyd steppe in after'. They all had to write their scripts (some no doubt brought with them), find suppliers and workmen, recruit and train the casts, organize the costumes and props, supervise the music and finally stage-manage the shows. Occasionally they took part themselves. As will be seen, plans had to be flexible, changes made and new material produced at very short notice as occasion demanded; much of their effort would be wasted. But at the end both Garter and Churchyard sounded well satisfied with the week's work.

Private citizens were also making their preparations for the great event, particularly those of some eminence in the county who would be taking part in the ceremonies. In July Nathaniel Bacon, younger son of the Lord Keeper, a Norfolk magistrate and, later, MP, was having a new velvet coat made. His friend and neighbour Christopher Heydon, who had evidently heard something of the unsettled state of the progress plans, added a PS to a letter dated 20 July (while the Queen was still at Havering) suggesting that if the coat were not finished, Bacon might delay it a little – 'for feare yt may somwhat be oute of fassyen [fashion] or ere Hir Highenes come if the byrde syng truly that I harde this day'.[3]

The Great Day

On Saturday 16 August, as recorded by Bernard Garter, who was there and who described her progress through the city in detail, 'Our most gratious soveraigne Lady Elizabeth by the grace of God Queen of England, France and Irelande, Defendor of the Faith etc. . . . our moste dread and soveraigne Lady . . . immediately after dinner set forward from Brakenashe . . . beeyng five myles distant from Norwich towards the same hir most dutifull Citie'. Garter seems to have stage-managed some of the happenings and certainly wrote some of the speeches.

As the Queen approached the city, from the other direction riding towards her came the Mayor and his procession. He was preceded by sixty 'Bachelers', the city's most 'comelie yong men', who had been bidden by the Mayor to attend attired as

¶ The receyuing of the Queenes Maiestie into hir highnesse Citie of Norvvich.

O N Saturday being the .rbj. of August. 1578. and in the twentith yere of the raigne of our most gratious soueraigne Lady Elizabeth by the grace of God Quēn of England, Fráce, and Irelande, Defendor of tho Faith. &c. The same our moste dread and soueraigne Lady (continuyng hir Progresse in Norffolke) immediately after dinner set forward from Brakenasshe; where she had dyned with the Ladye Style, beeyng fiue myles distant from Norwich; towardes the same hir most dutifull Citie : Sir Robert Wood, then Esquire, and nowe Knight, Maior of the same Citie, at one of the Clocke the same happy day, sette forwarde to mēete with hir Maiestie in this order : Firste there roade before him wel and sēmely mounted, threescore of the most comelie yong men of the Citie, as Bachelers, apparelled all in blacke Sattyn doublets, blacke Hose, blacke Taffata Hattes and yeallowe Bandes, and their vniuersall linerie was a Mandylion of purple Taffata, layde aboute with siluer Lace : and so apparelled, marched forwardes two and two in a ranke. Then one whiche represented King G V R G V N T, sometyme King of Englande, whiche buylded the Castle of Norwich, called Blanch Flowre, and layde the foundation of the Citie . He was mounted vppon a braue Courser, and was thus furnished : His body Ar-

A. iij.   med,

The opening page of Bernard Garter's account of the Queen's visit to Norwich, 'The receyving of the Queenes Maiestie'.

instructed, on pain of a 40s fine.[4] They wore black satin doublets, black hose, black taffeta hats with yellow bands and purple taffeta mandelions (long jackets with hanging sleeves and open seams) decorated with silver lace. They were followed by 'a noble companye of gentlemen and wealthie citizens in velvet coates', among them no doubt Nathaniel Bacon. Then came the officers of the city: the sword-bearer, the Mayor, twenty-four aldermen and the Recorder in scarlet gowns, and former city sheriffs in violet gowns and satin stoles. Finally, there came officers to keep back the crowds. They had left the city centre at one o'clock and now reached the boundary, Harford Bridge over the River Yare, where they all waited for an hour or so.

At last the Queen and her procession came into sight and such were the shouts and cheers from the waiting crowd that 'hardly for a great time coulde anything be hearde'. When eventually the noise died down the Mayor greeted the Queen with a welcoming speech in Latin (recorded and translated by Garter), the sword of the city and a silver and gilt cup containing £100 in gold. The Queen replied with a short speech of thanks, adding rather disingenuously that she had not come for gifts – 'Princes have no neede of money, God hath endowed us abundantly' – but for the hearts and allegiance of her subjects. Nevertheless, the cup having been handed to a gentleman to carry, the Mayor seems to have thought it prudent to make sure that she was aware of the contents and said to the Queen, 'Sunt hic centum librae puri auri.' Whereupon, the lid of the cup was raised and, perhaps in case he had not understood the Mayor's Latin, she said to the gentleman carrying it, 'Looke to it, there is a hundreth pound.'

In addition to these formalities, there was an unofficial interlude at Hartford Bridge. Edward Downes, Lord of the Manor of Earlham, 2 or 3 miles up the river, appeared, no doubt suitably escorted, with the intention of clarifying his tenure of the manor which he had acquired as recently as 1571. He was apparently allowed to deliver a set of verses in archaic English, declaring that he held the manor from the Queen in return for a pair of spurs. He was also under an obligation to perform the duties of Lieutenant and High Constable of the Castle during her stay, in lieu of which he had to pay £3 a year to the Crown, but he was to receive 'the palfrey which thy maiestie [majesty] doe beare'. In conclusion he declaimed:

> Lo, thus to thee his whole state is known
> whos hart and land and goods are all thy own.

He then presented the Queen with a pair of gold spurs;[5] it seems very unlikely that she gave him her horse in return. Neither Churchyard nor Garter mentions this intervention, which was evidently outside the planned programme.

Edward Downes seems to have consulted a legal relative in London about his intention to make this appearance, because he was afraid that if he were found to owe the Crown any duty when the Queen came, his estate would be in jeopardy. The cousin advised against such a step; if he called attention to any obligation, it would be on record and so inescapable.[6] Some years later Downes must have regretted that he had not taken this sensible advice: he was forced to apply to be let off his contribution of 'a light horse' to the county's muster of arms on the grounds that his house had blown down, he was in debt and he was already paying his £3 a year in lieu of service at the castle.[7]

Eventually the whole assembly moved off towards the city, the Queen preceded by the Mayor carrying the mace. At the Town Close outside the city walls a legendary figure, King Gurgant, who was believed to have built the Castle Blanche Flower in Norwich, stepped forward. He was in armour over green and white silk with a black velvet hat trimmed with white feathers and was attended by three henchmen also in green and white. He had ready a speech in verse, evidently written by Garter, but a sudden shower forced the Queen to carrying on without stopping and Gurgant's speech became the first of several that she was not to hear.

The procession now approached St Stephen's Gate, which had been not only repaired as the Assembly had ordered but decorated on the outside with the Queen's arms and badge, flanked by St George's cross and the city arms, and on the inside the Tudor rose between the roses of York and Lancaster (whose white and red colours were, oddly, reversed in Garter's account) and below them the Queen's arms again. As Elizabeth passed through, she heard the first burst of music from the City Waits in their new or refurbished uniforms.

The five Waits were an important and colourful part of the mayor's entourage, retained and paid by the city to play when required. They carried a painted and fringed banner and their wind instruments – shawms, hautboys, sackbuts and recorders – were adorned with small flags. They wore silver chains and badges, some of which have survived. The Norwich Waits were famous and in 1589 Sir Francis Drake took them with him on an expedition against Portugal (they had to leave their chains behind). Those who went included two of the five who entertained the Queen during her visit to Norwich; one, Peter Spratt, returned, but sadly Robert Thacker and two others died on the voyage.[8]

In St Stephen's Street a stage had been built with a painted backdrop showing looms and weavers making the various kinds of fabric that Norwich produced. On the stage itself were sixteen 'small women children', eight spinning yarn for worsted and eight knitting worsted yarn hose, and men holding samples of their products. In the middle was 'a prettie boy richly apparelled' who declaimed a poem by Garter explaining the exhibition. All this pleased the Queen. She was probably especially interested in the stocking knitters, though she herself wore silk, having been given a pair in 1561 and decided there and then never to wear woven cloth stockings again. She thanked the participants warmly before moving off to the market-place.

At the end of the street leading into the market an elaborate gateway had been constructed, with three archways; above there were another stage and two little rooms

St Stephen's Gate, through which the Queen entered Norwich (artist's impression of the gate decorated as described by Bernard Garter).

for the musicians. The surfaces were painted to look like jasper and marble and again were decorated with the arms of England and the Queen's own badge, a falcon bearing the crown and sceptre. On the other side, facing the market, were the arms and crest of England. When the Queen came into sight, music was heard from the players above the postern gates. When it stopped, a rather curious mix of allegorical and biblical figures, the city of Norwich, Deborah, Judith, Esther and Martia, each welcomed her with verses written by Garter, and the musicians and 'the best voyces in the citie' sang a song by Churchyard which expressed joy at the Queen's coming and was called 'The deaw of heaven'. One charming verse began:

> The sunne doth shine where shade hath bin
> Long darknesse brought us day,
> The starre of comfort now coms in,
> And heere awhile will stay.

The Norwich City Waits' silver-gilt chains, 1535, to be seen in Norwich City Guildhall. The links represent the castle and lion from the Norwich coat of arms.

At the end the Queen passed through the gate into the market-place and the musicians started up again with a song by Garter about a dream of gods and goddesses, ending, rather prosaically, when he woke:

> The world and they concluded with a breath,
> And wisht long raign to Queene Elizabeth.

Finally, as she rode through the decorated streets towards the cathedral, the Queen came to another stage set up in a churchyard (perhaps St Andrew's or the former Blackfriars, which was almost opposite) on which Churchyard had placed 'an excellent boy . . . in a long white roabe of taffata', wearing a red and gold turban and a garland of flowers. The Queen's attention was caught by some music 'marvellous sweete and good', in spite, complained Churchyard, of some interference by the 'rudeness of some ringer of belles'. When she halted, the boy stepped forward and made a little speech in verse beginning rather apologetically:

> Great things were meant to welcome thee, O Queene,
> If want of time had not cut off the same.

(Evidently Churchyard had not found his three weeks in Norwich long enough.) At his conclusion, 'Thine owne we are in heart, in word and deede', the boy threw up his garland and Elizabeth said, 'This device is fine.' The music started up again and she paused a good while to listen. Eventually, however, she moved on and arrived at the cathedral, which, said Churchyard, 'was not farre from thence'.

The cathedral authorities, like the city, had made elaborate preparations to receive the Queen. Outside in the precinct, paths and the waterway down to Pulls Ferry were cleaned, dungheaps were removed, animals shut up, walls whitewashed and broken glass replaced. The Erpingham Gate was decorated and the roadway through it cleaned up. Inside, the coats of arms were repainted, including those of the Queen's ancestors Lady Anne Boleyn, great-grandmother of Queen Anne Boleyn, and Sir William Boleyn, her grandfather. A great throne was made, the canopy stiffened with buckram and covered and hung with crimson velvet, satin and silk and decorated with crimson silk lace and a dozen silk buttons. The cushions took eight leather skins.[9]

Gentleman Usher Anthony Wingfeld had also spent two days at the cathedral making ready for Her Majesty, checking perhaps that the Dean's preparations were appropriate.

The Queen and the Court with the Mayor and the city dignitaries arrived in the evening to hear a Te Deum sung. With both processions and the Bishop and all his priests and officers, the cathedral must have been full. The Queen's throne was on the north side of the high altar in front of the reliquary arch and almost opposite the tomb of her Boleyn ancestors (which she would have readily recognized from the heraldic devices).

The music came from a new organ recently installed. Among the singers would have been eight lay clerks or 'Singing Men' including Osbert Parsley (or Parslove), a singer and composer, whose memorial tablet records fifty years in the cathedral ending with his death in 1585. It includes the line 'Whose Harmony survives his vital Breath', and indeed some of his music still exists and is sung occasionally in the cathedral. Parsley was paid $6s$ $8d$ by the cathedral authorities 'for the songs composed and sung by him' while the Queen was in Norwich.[10]

At some point the Dean and prebends presented the Queen with a casket lined with crimson velvet and containing £20 in gold. They also spent £14 $4s$ $8d$ in gifts and payments to her officials and servants, including $20s$ to Anthony Wingfeld and

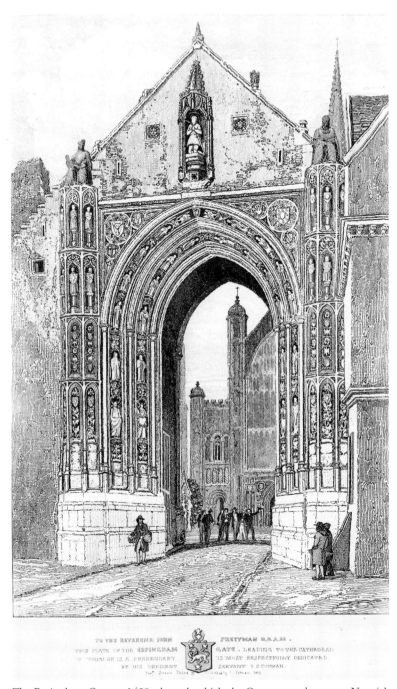

The Erpingham Gate, *c*. 1420, through which the Queen passed to enter Norwich Cathedral (etching John Sell Cotman, 1817).

his team and 10*s* to Raphe Hope and his men. They paid the City Waits 6*s*. In all, the Queen's stay cost them about £35.[11]

After the service the Queen retired to the Bishop's Palace, where she was to stay and which Anthony Wingfeld and his men had prepared for her. It is possible that even the Bishop had to move out while she was there. Probably Lord Burghley also stayed at the palace. Lord Leicester stayed at the Dean's house, which was also in the precinct.[12]

Some time on that busy Saturday someone found a moment to arrange the payment, authorized at Kenninghall, of £50 to Robert Gascoigne for the postal service which had been ordered by the Council at Havering. The Post Master himself was evidently not there; perhaps he had escorted the Lord of Dunfermline back to Scotland. No other business is recorded on that day.

The Queen's Week

The next day, Sunday, seems to have been a much-needed rest day for almost everybody. Churchyard remarked piously that on Sunday, 'Princes commonly come not abroade and tyme is occupied with sermons and laudable exercises', though in fact on the previous Sunday the Queen had been watching the country dancing at Euston when the incriminating statue of the Virgin was found. However, as far as the evidence goes, only Lord Treasurer Burghley continued to work on this Sunday, when he studied and occasionally amended a list prepared by his officers giving the names of 324 Norfolk gentlemen with the locations of their houses.[13] It was clearly difficult for anyone of note to escape the Council's attention.

On Monday the weather was bad and the Queen stayed indoors. There will have been business for her to attend to, including at least some of the items on the agenda of the Privy Council, which met that day; all eight regular members attended. They discussed, as always, affairs in the Low Countries and the situation in Scotland, which now looked serious – the rebellious Scottish lords were threatening to attack Morton. The Queen, 'graciously tendering the dangerous state of the young King' and putting expedient before the scruples she had entertained at Audley End, promised armed support for James VI if he should need it. Lord Hunsdon, who had left the progress at Audley End, had already been sent north to assemble and arm forces to assist him, 'in case any violence shall be offered him by his disobedient servants'. James had made a gesture of friendship towards Elizabeth in sending her some falcons and Hunsdon suggested to Lord Burghley that she in turn should 'remember hym with some token'.[14]

By now the Sheriff of Pembrokeshire had appeared before the Council. He was required to put down a bond of £200 and was then allowed to go home, making the long journey back to Wales, only to return a couple of months later to fulfil the Council's condition for his release. He had to present himself before the Star Chamber in London within ten days of the Feast of All Saints, 1 November.

Several letters were dispatched to envoys and agents in the Low Countries. One was carried by Nynyan Cockbourne, 'Scoteshman', who would be back in about a month's time. Six of the Council signed a formal letter to the ambassadors, Lord Cobham and Sir Francis Walsingham, which reached them at Louvain six days later. Mr Secretary Wilson wrote separately to Walsingham. Apparently the Queen's habitual vacillations had been causing them trouble again and Lord Leicester had taken her to task. Wilson reported admiringly that 'he dealt so plainly, so boldly and so faithfully . . . with our sovereign against delays and unnecessary used allegations as I never heard councillor take the like upon him'. Fortunately for Leicester, 'he was heard with as great patience' as he had used. Wilson also commented on Saturday's events in Norwich: 'never was sovereign more princely received than the Queen has been here'. But the Council remained concerned for the safety of the realm and Wilson added, 'in the midst of all this jollity it were good to provide for mischief hereafter'.

But Monday was not wholly filled with business. In the evening before supper Churchyard put on a dramatic display to tempt the Queen to come out and 'see what pastyme the Gods had provided for a noble Prince'. He had covered a coach – itself a rarity in Norwich at that time – with cut-outs of birds, sprites and clouds attached so that they quivered, and built on it a gilt and bejewelled tower topped with a plume of spangled white feathers. It was drawn by painted and winged horses and driven by a coachman 'sutable to the same'. In it rode a trumpeter and Mercury, messenger of the gods, in blue satin slashed and lined with gold, with wings on his matching peaked hat and on his heels. He carried a golden rod, also winged, its two serpents wriggling as it moved. The coach had been hidden until the right moment came. Then, as it came into the cathedral close, the coachman had orders to drive as fast as he could so 'the horses should seeme to flye'. The trumpeter sounded his horn and the coach swept into Green Yard between the Bishop's Palace and the cathedral. It drew up before the window of what was now the Privy Chamber and the Queen, presumably forewarned, came to where she could easily be seen. Mercury jumped down, gave a little skip or two and advanced so bravely 'that the Queene smiled at the boldnesse of the boy'. Then he bowed, shook his golden rod and delivered a long speech in verse describing his mission from Jehova to Elizabeth. He was to:

> Tell hir that she is to me so deere
> That I appoynt by man's device and arte
> That every day she shall see sundrie shoes [shows]
> If that she please to walke and take the ayre;
> And that so soone as oute of doore she goes
> (If time do serve and weather waxeth fayre)
> Some odd device shall meete hir Highnesse streight
> To make hir smyle and ease her burthened brest. . . .

The speech, said Churchyard, was 'very well taken and understood' by the Queen, who 'will not have anye thing duetifully offred to passe unregarded'. Mercury left as he arrived, watched by the marvelling crowds, who had followed him into the close. That day the 'devisor' was well satisfied with his work.

On Tuesday the weather seems to have improved and early in the morning the Queen rode out of the city to hunt in Lady Jerningham's 1,000 acre deer park at Costessey, 2 or 3 miles beyond St Benet's Gate along the road towards King's Lynn. Earlier in the century the manor had belonged to Henry VIII, who had granted it to Anne of Cleves. By 1547 it had reverted to the Crown and Mary Tudor gave it to her Vice-Chamberlain, Sir Henry Jerningham. He died in 1571, leaving it to his widow.[15] It was in this lady's house that Elizabeth had dinner. Anthony Wingfeld spent two days there working on 'a dyning house' for her. When in 1622 an inventory of the contents of the thirty-seven or so rooms was made, in the long gallery was 'a great chair covered with red velvet and laced with gold lace'[16] – just the thing for the Queen's seat at the dinner. Charles Smythe, Page of Her Majesty's Robes, came for the one day; the Queen would have needed a change of costume for hunting.

Clearly Elizabeth had come for the sport, certainly not to honour her involuntary hostess. Lady Jerningham was known to have Catholic sympathies and, as the widow of an official of Mary Tudor, was inevitably suspect. Indeed, her name had appeared on a list of recusants drawn up by the bishop the previous year.[17] However, perhaps because of her age, no harm befell her following the royal visit, though she had connections with several families whose recusant members were summoned by the Council during the progress; two years later her granddaughter was to marry the son of Suffolk recusant Edmund Bedingfeld. Her son-in-law Charles Walgrave, although summoned to Norwich by the Council, was also to escape their further attention. When she died in 1583, Lady Jerningham's will provided for Joane, her own fool and for another 'poore foole' maintained in her son's household;[18] the family was traditionalist not only in religion.

A priest who had been her son's schoolmaster and was still a member of her household, 'Mr Dereham', also attracted the Council's attention. He was summoned to appear before them in Norwich but, whether by chance or forewarned, he had left Norfolk in time and apparently gone to Buxton Spa. The following week the fanatical Topclyffe, who had been in Norwich, wrote to the Earl of Shrewsbury, who owned the medicinal springs and had built a bath-house with accommodation for visitors there. Topclyffe claimed that the Queen had told him of certain Papists who had gone to Buxton after Lord Leicester had left. They included 'a detestable Popish priest, one Dyrham or Durande', whom Topclyffe remembered 'at the bathe or lurking in those partts after the ladyes'. The Council had written to Lord Shrewsbury asking him to apprehend and question Dereham: 'upon the least or lightest occasion' he was to be imprisoned and the Council informed.[19] Again Dereham seems to have escaped. On

14 September the Council, well on their way back to London, informed the Bishop of Norwich that he had now returned to Norfolk and was 'attendant for the most part about the Lady Jerningham's'. The Bishop was to arrest and imprison him 'for that he is suspected to be one that useth to saie Masse and to use bad practises to the disturbance of the common quiett of this realm'. At some point Lady Jerningham seems to have made some show of religious conformity, for many years later Dereham was said to have frightened the old lady by saying that in receiving Protestant communion she had brought damnation upon herself.[20]

On her way out of the city towards Costessey, the Queen encountered the first of Churchyard's major 'shows'. He had had some difficulty in getting together all he needed, but he persisted in spite of discouragement and defections, aware that time was passing and 'dayes and houres did wast (without doying anything promised)'. In haste he assembled his 'boyes and men with al their furnitures' in two coaches and set out for the open ground outside St Benet's Gate, followed again by a great crowd of common people, as many, he said, as came with the Queen when she emerged. Garter describes the production as 'a very prety pleasant shew' and Churchyard records it fully. Again it involved figures of classical mythology, Venus and Cupid, and allegories such as Chastitie, Modestie and Temperance in conflict with Wantonesse and Ryot in a complex plot. A song sung by her 'wayting maydes' praised Chastitie and complimented the Virgin Queen:

> Chast life lives long and lookes on worlde and wicked ways;
> Chaste life for loss of pleasures short doth winne immortall prayse. . .
> Lewd life cuttes off his dayes and soone runnes out his date,
> Confounds good wits, breeds naughty bloud and weakens mans estate.

A speech by Modestie praising Elizabeth ended rather uninspiringly:

> So, gay and glittring Dame, thy graces are not small,
> Thy heavenly gifts in greatest prease, in deede surmounts them all.

At the end, said Churchyard, he had 'gracious words . . . openly and often pronounced by Hir Highnesse'.

As she returned to the city, the minister of the Dutch church, representing the immigrant workers, was given the opportunity to present the Queen with yet another cup, worth, said Garter, £50. It was later recorded by the Court officials as 'a faire standing bolle with a cover of silver guilt' weighing 108 oz.[21] The Dutchmen had been given the use of part of the former church of the Black Friars. This was on her route from St Benet's Gate back to the Bishop's Palace, so the minister may well have been stationed outside his own church to make his presentation. Inside the cup was engraved a verse with a curious reference to Elizabeth's imprisonment by her sister Mary Tudor nearly twenty-five years earlier:

> So thee, O Queene, the Lord hath ledd
> from prison and deceite
> Of thine, unto these highest toppes
> of your princely estate.

In offering the cup, the minister gave an oration in Latin (Garter recorded both Latin and English texts). In it he expressed his compatriots' appreciation of their life in Norwich, tactfully ignoring the local opposition to their presence, which as recently as 1570 had led to an armed rising against the city government. Perhaps there had been a change of attitude, for 'we give immortall thanks', he said, 'for these thy singuler benefits of godlinesse towards us and that we live under so good a tutor beeing magistrate in this the Citie of Norwich . . . and that we find the mindes of the people favourable towards us'.

It may have been on this day, when the Queen was occupied outside the city, that Lord Burghley and Lord Leicester rode off to Yarmouth. The town had been led to expect the Queen herself – it had been visited by William Bowles – and preparations had been made for her arrival. She was to be met by the aldermen in scarlet robes and the commoners in black. The servants of the Bailiffs, Yarmouth's chief officers, were to have new uniforms and the aldermen's servants were to wear black lined with white. The bridge over the River Yare was strengthened.[22] But the Queen did not come, according to some accounts because of the plague, and Yarmouth had to make do with Lord Burghley and Lord Leicester (who was High Steward of Yarmouth), who arrived with a train of 500 gentlemen. They were received by the two Bailiffs and twelve aldermen with great rejoicing by the townsfolk and an entertainment and feast. As they left they heard a speech by the Sheriff and were given three gilt bowls with covers valued at 100 marks (£66 13s 4d) to take to the Queen.[23] Earlier the Yarmouth MP, William le Grice, had been asked to buy for the town a silver cup in the form of a ship to be given to the Queen;[24] nothing seems to have come of this for only the three gilt bowls were subsequently recorded as 'Geven by the township of Yermouth' during the progress.[25] The councillors also found time to inspect the harbour and no doubt heard the complaints of the fishing industry about their neighbours at Gorleston. Yarmouth must have been disappointed not to receive the Queen herself, but they made the best of the occasion and their hospitality and arguments were to be rewarded when the Council reached Thetford.

Yet another Frenchman reached the Court that Tuesday. The Venetian ambassador in Paris had reported to his masters on 10 August that Nicholas Angennes, Sieur de Rambouillet, a special ambassador sent from the King of France to Elizabeth, had already left for England.[26] According to Secretary Wilson, he was coming 'to advance the match [of the Queen with Alençon] as much as may be'.

On the Wednesday the Queen and the French envoys dined at Surrey House, just outside the city, across the river from Bishops Gate. Anthony Wingfeld had spent two days there, as he had at Lady Jerningham's, setting up a dining house. At the Dissolution of the Monasteries the Priory of St Leonard had been given by Henry VIII to the 3rd Duke of Norfolk, whose son, the Earl of Surrey, built a house there. After his execution in 1547, it reverted to the Crown, but in 1562 Elizabeth gave it to his son, the 4th Duke.[27] He in his turn was executed in 1572, but, as with Kenninghall, his son Philip, another Earl of Surrey, seems to have retained his property. He had evidently come on with the progress from Kenninghall to his Norwich house, where, said Churchyard, the Queen and the Court were given 'a moste rare and delicate dinner and banquette'. They crossed the river in barges, no doubt prepared as the mayor had instructed some weeks before.

Churchyard had planned to put on a 'shewe' for the Queen on her way back into the city, so he and his men assembled by the river between 'my Lord of Surrey's backedore' and her waiting barge. Here they found themselves with too little space, so they all got into boats and waited by the landing stage to which the Queen would come. With everything ready they 'hoovered on the water three long houres'. Still the royal party did not come and it was getting dark. Eventually they gave up and went home. Garter, referring to this disappointing outcome, blamed the weather.

When finally the Queen did return, her way passed the Great Hospital, where, at the door, stood Stephen Limbert, master of the grammar school, ready with a speech. The grammar school was housed in the old chantry, above the medieval charnel house to the west of the cathedral; in preparation for her visit $9s$ $4d$ had been spent on painting the door and cleaning up the surroundings, including the removal of three loads of 'street muck'. Limbert had already taught at the school for fifteen years and had been master since 1569. When the Queen came, he was about thirty-two and was to live and work there for another twenty years, dying, as his (now lost) brass memorial said, 'full of Dayes and of Comfort in the Multitude and Proficiencie of his Scholars'.[28]

Evidently as the Queen approached he looked nervous, for she greeted him with 'Be not afrayed'. Emboldened, he was able both to thank her for her 'good encouragement' and to deliver his Latin speech (quoted in full and translated by Garter). As he began, the Queen called to the three French envoys and the English dignitaries who were with her and told them to listen. She herself was very attentive all through the oration. At the end, when she had thanked Master Limbert, she added generously, 'It is the best that I ever heard' and, pulling off her glove, she gave him her hand. Limbert, properly coached, perhaps by Garter, went on one knee, then rose and kissed the offered hand. The Queen moved on, but when she was back in the palace she sent someone to find out his name. There was no other entertainment that night.

It may have been this day, when she was accompanied by the French party, that Elizabeth presented one of them, a 'Mons Plasses', with a gold chain.[29] The gift seems to have been made on impulse, perhaps for some small personal service, for the Queen 'borrowed' the chain from Edward Stafford, one of her Gentlemen Pensioners, who was attached to de Bacqueville's party for their stay in England. The chain was part of his insignia, so she would have known that it was conveniently to hand.

On that Wednesday there was a meeting of the Council with the usual eight members. Among their business was a report received from the commissioners responsible for the government of London that evidence of witchcraft had been found in the city; it was accompanied by three wax images. In reply the Council instructed the Lord Mayor, the Lord Bishop, Sir William Cordell, Master of the Rolls (evidently now back in London) and others to use 'secret means' to locate the people involved. Less than three weeks later and well before the end of the progress, Ambassador Mendoza in London was able to describe the wax figures which had been hidden in a stable. They were, he told Madrid, two spans (about 12 inches) high, the middle one with 'Elizabeth' across its forehead and the others dressed like two of her ministers. They were stuck with pigs' bristles. The Queen had been worried by the find, but in spite of intensive inquiries nothing had been discovered so far.[30]

The next day, Thursday, the Queen herself told Churchyard that she wanted to see 'what pastimes were prepared' for her. In the morning Lord Chamberlain Sussex warned him that she would go out in the afternoon and ordered him to have something ready for her to see. Churchyard made elaborate and ingenious preparations. Knowing which way she would go, he took over an area 20 yards square in which he had a great hole dug and covered with a green canvas which could be opened and shut by means of cords running through rings. In this 'cave' he stationed musicians and twelve 'water nymphs' in long robes made of white silk or linen and covered with rushes. They carried bunches of bulrushes and wore wreaths of ivy and moss over the golden wigs which covered their shoulders and reached down to their waists. They looked so beautiful that even those who knew the boys could hardly recognize them and some people even 'tooke them to be yong girles and wenches'. The plan was that, as the Queen approached, four of the nymphs should 'poppe up out of the cave' in turn and deliver a rhyming – though somewhat unpoetic – speech, the first concluding:

> And hearing that there came a Queen along this water side,
> So long as we poore silly nimphes on land dare well abide,
> We daunce, we hop and bounse it up in honor of hir name,
> To whom Diana and hir trayne doth give immortal fame.

At the end of the fourth speech calling the nymphs back into their cave, 'It is a shame for water nimphs on earth so long to rest', they would disappear as the canvas was pulled over their heads and music would come 'secretely and strangely out of the earth'. Finally all twelve nymphs would emerge and perform a dance with 'timbrels'. These tambourine-like instruments had apparently fallen out of use and were unfamiliar at the time. Churchyard's were trimmed with 'belles and other iangling things' and made such a 'confused noyse' that the hearers were amazed by 'that new-founde toy'.

At the same time a group of men and the boy who was to play 'Beautie' were ready to put on an allegorical play in which Manhode (Manliness), Favour (Comeliness) and Dezarte (Excellence) struggle with Good Fortune for the hand of the Lady Beautie. The final scene was to be a battle in which 'legges and armes of men (well and lively wrought)' were to fall to the ground 'as bloudy as might be'.

Again Churchyard was unfortunate. Just when the Queen was due to come to her coach and her courtiers were ready to mount their horses, a thunderstorm broke over their heads and the players were forced to seek shelter. The 'cave' was close to the river – surprisingly – and Churchyard and some others got into a boat under a bridge, but 'we were all so dashed and washed that it was a greater pastime to see us looke like drowned rattes' than the best of his shows. All the velvets, silks, tinsel and cloth of gold were wasted and, as Churchyard said, having been cut out for these costumes, would not be much use afterwards. Nevertheless, he was philosophical about the difficulty of performing in the open air, quoting the old saying 'that men doth purpose and God dothe dispose'.

He might have been comforted to know that in the following March, the City Chamberlains were authorized to sell what they could of 'the apparel and other stuff and thinges that were prepared for shewes ageynst the Queen's comying'; at least some of the expenditure was recovered.[31]

Some time during the day the French king's ambassador, who had arrived on Tuesday, had an audience with the Queen. No doubt the question of the Alençon marriage was brought up.

In the evening after supper the Queen watched a masque in her Privy Chamber in the Bishop's Palace. The entertainment seems to have been offered by the Mayor on behalf of the city, though it was written by Henry Goldingham, who, with Garter, had followed Churchyard to Norwich; it was recorded in full in Garter's account.

It opened with another appearance by Mercury, presumably Churchyard's lad from Monday. He was followed by two torch-bearers whose costumes, purple taffeta mandelions trimmed with silver lace, bore a marked resemblance to those of the 'Bachelers' who had accompanied the Mayor when he met the Queen at the city limits the previous Saturday; probably they were some of the same comely young men. With them came five musicians in long white silk robes with garlands on their

A masque – pairs of symbolic figures parade around the room (detail from *The Life of Sir Henry Unton*, *c.* 1596, artist unknown).

heads. Then came pairs of classical figures, Jupiter and Juno, Mars and Venus, Apollo and Pallas, and Neptune and Diana, with more torch-bearers and finally Cupid. The characters each delivered a speech and presented the Queen with a gift. These included 'a ryding wande of whales fin curiously wrought' from Jupiter; 'a fayre payre of knyves' from Mars; and a white dove from Venus which when set free 'ranne directly to the Queene and, being taken uppe and set uppon the table before Hir Majestie, sate so quietly as if it had been tied'. Apollo presented a musical instrument which he played and sang to and Neptune gave 'a noble pike' hidden in the belly of 'a great artificiall fishe'. Finally Cupid offered a golden arrow with a speech in verse, possibly written with the marriage negotiations in mind:

> This is of Golde, meete for the noblest Queene
> Wherefore Dame faire, take thou this gift of me . . .
> Shoot but this shaft at King or Caesar: He,
> And he is thine . . .

The Queen received the gifts with thanks; the actors performed a final parade around the room and left.

When they had gone the Queen summoned Mayor Robert Wood and thanked him. Then she took him by the hand and spoke to him privately. 'And thus', said Garter, 'this delightfull night passed to the ioy of all whiche sawe hir Grace in so plesaunt plight [mood].'

Some time during the week the Queen received yet another gift from local citizens, this time brought over from King's Lynn. On 6 August, while the progress was still at Bury St Edmunds, the Mayor, aldermen and Common Council had met and agreed 'to sheawe there dutifull obedience and good wills' with a gift of 100 angels (gold coins) if Lord Leicester, who was High Steward of Lynn as well as Yarmouth, and the town's Recorder approved. As a first step £45 10s was taken out of the treasury and given to the Mayor. A week later two townsmen were sent off to seek the necessary advice at Stanfeld Hall near Bracon Ash, where, conveniently, Lord Leicester was staying with Edward Flowerdew, their Recorder.[32] Finally, a delegation from Lynn reached the Queen at Norwich and presented her with the money in a purse decorated with pearl and gold.[33]

'Frowning Friday'

The next day, Friday, saw the end of this momentous visit. In the morning the Queen performed her last official duty, the knighting of five Norfolk gentlemen in the Great Hall of the Bishop's Palace. If this was the old hall built in the early part of the fourteenth century by Bishop Salmon, it was an imposing size, 120 by 60 ft.[34] The men so honoured varied considerably in their interests and leanings.

Only one, Edward Clere of Blickling, was directly involved in the progress; Elizabeth was to stay in his house in Thetford a few days later. A member of an old Norfolk family and distantly related to the Queen through their common great-grandfather Sir William Boleyn, he was, at the age of about forty, a great landowner and very wealthy. At different times in his life an MP and a magistrate, his main objective was to carry out the Council's policy in his county, paying little regard to local interests. He was consequently not popular with his Norfolk neighbours.

Thomas Knyvett of Ashwellthorpe also came from an eminent Norfolk family and was about the same age as Clere. He owned great estates too. In religion he seems to have leaned towards Puritanism and his main concerns lay with the local community.

He was a magistrate and for a few years Deputy Lieutenant of the County, but he was also much interested in his considerable library (many of his books survive in the Cambridge University Library) and collection of antiques. His hospitality to the poor was legendary.

Raphe Shelton of Shelton, about 10 miles south of Norwich, was a neighbour of Knyvett and also came a family long established in Norfolk. Like Clere, he was related to Elizabeth, his grandmother having been a Boleyn of Blickling, aunt to Queen Anne, but his father had supported Mary Tudor and the family was not greatly in favour with the Queen. He was a conservative in religion and politics and had been a supporter of the executed Duke of Norfolk. His interests seem to have been entirely local; at this time he had been a magistrate for over ten years. He was probably older than the others and was to die two years later.

William Paston came from another ancient family, remembered now for the Paston letters, written in the fifteenth century. Their home, at Paston near the north Norfolk coast, had been visited by William Bowles on his fact-finding mission before the progress started, but it was never used by the Queen. Eminent in local affairs, he was a magistrate almost all his long life – aged fifty when he was knighted, he lived to be eighty-two. Another former supporter of the Duke, he inclined to conservatism and had accepted the new religion without enthusiasm.

Nicholas Bacon was the eldest son of Elizabeth's Lord Keeper Bacon and brother of Nathaniel, who had the new velvet coat. The Bacons were a recently advanced family who became important county figures in the sixteenth century. Nicholas lived at Redgrave, on the Suffolk border, and his main sphere of influence was in that county, though he was appointed a Norfolk magistrate in the year of his knighthood when he was about thirty-five and continued on the bench to the end of the century. A man of uncompromising character and legal background, in religion he held Puritan beliefs.[35]

On this last day the Queen dined in Norwich and set off in the afternoon towards Kimberley Hall, her next lodging. Schoolmaster Limbert, encouraged perhaps by her kindness on the previous Wednesday, had prepared another Latin speech to deliver at the Queen's departure, probably as she left the Bishop's Palace. Unfortunately, she was late in leaving and there was no time for the oration, though the text was handed to her. It was also printed in both Latin and English by Garter.

Garter describes the streets on her way as hung from side to side with 'cordes made of hearbes and floures' and lavishly decorated with garlands, pictures and banners. At the city gate a stage had been built, covered in cloth of gold and crimson velvet, on which were a group of hidden musicians and Garter himself. When the Queen and her entourage arrived below him, he came forward with a speech in verse beginning:

> Terrestrial ioyes are tyed wih sclender file
> Eche happy hap full hastily doth slyde.

At the end Elizabeth, as usual, thanked the performer and then listened to the song written by Garter and sung, he said, 'in a very sweete voice', probably by one of the musicians. It began:

> What vayleth life where sorrowe soakes the harte?

Eventually the procession rode out through the gate in the city walls. Garter called it St Benet's Gate but this would not have led to the road to Earlham Bridge, where the final ceremonies took place, or to Kimberley. It is much more likely that Elizabeth left via St Giles's Gate, where the roadway had been improved in preparation for the visit. Before they reached the limits of the city land, however, they came upon Churchyard and his final entertainment.

Once again he had had problems with his helpers. 'Myne aydes', he said, 'were drawn from me.' Determined to do something that might make the Queen laugh, he called together the boys who should have been the water nymphs the day before and converted them into fairies. They all drove out of the city along the progress route and set themselves up in a field behind some high bushes. There the seven brightest of the boys had to learn new parts and put on their nymph costumes. As the Queen came up to their hiding place, they emerged through the hedge and each delivered a verse, the third saying:

> Yea out of hedge we crept indeed where close in caves we lay,
> And knowing by the brute of fame a Queene must passe this way,
> To make her laugh we clapt on coates of segges [rushes] and bulrush both
> That she shuld know and world should say Lo there the Phayries goth.

As Churchyard hoped, the Queen did indeed smile and laugh and he himself, in a water-sprite costume, emerged and led all twelve boys in a dance with his special tambourines. As the dancers retired the Queen moved off, having, said Churchyard, 7 miles to go. It was then five o'clock.

After 2 miles the procession reached Earlham Bridge, where the River Yare again marked the city boundary. Here Mayor Robert Wood expected to make a final oration. However, according to Garter, it was then seven o'clock and there were still 5 miles to ride. Lord Chamberlain Sussex therefore advised against another speech, although the Mayor was allowed to hand the Queen copies of his Latin and English texts. She thanked him and all the aldermen and commoners for their generous entertainment and for their hospitality to her followers. Then she called the Mayor to her and in a last formal ceremony knighted him. Finally she said, 'I have laid up in my breast such good wil as I shall never forget Norwich' and rode away, shaking her riding crop and saying with tears in her eyes, 'Farewel, Norwich.'

Lord North and his son must have left some time earlier in the day to ride the 50-odd miles home to Kirtling. John, who was not provided for by the Court, had had to pay his own way. The round trip via Euston, Kenninghall and Bracon Ash cost him £1 16s 2d. Most of it went on the horses and his men; the rent of his room in Norwich for the week was 5s – no doubt prices were somewhat inflated.

A final generous gesture from the Queen came during the following week when she sent Henry Sackford, a gentleman of the Privy Chamber, back to Norwich with £30 in aid for the 'poor straungers'. The leaders of the Dutch and Walloon communities were called into the Mayor's Court to witness the handing over of the money to four deacons, two from each group; the Dutch received £19 and the Walloons £11.[36] Perhaps the Queen had been touched by the immigrants' gift of a cup on the previous Tuesday.

The visit had cost the cathedral authorities and the city a good deal more. In addition to their gift to the Queen and the cost of the 'shows' put on by Churchyard and Garter, the city officers spent £36 6s 8d on gifts to the royal servants. The Gentlemen Ushers, presumably Anthony Wingfeld and some of his men, received £2 (in addition to their 20s from the Dean), the two Grooms of the Chamber, who were part of Wingfeld's team, got £1 and the four Harbingers who had come earlier £1 6s 8d. Others who were tipped included the man who carried 'the Cittie Sword' from Hartford Bridge when the Queen arrived and to Earlham Bridge when she left, waiters, porters, messengers, 'cooks and boylors', the Surveyor of the Waies (roads), officers of the buttery and the cellar, heralds (who got £5) and four groups of musicians, trumpeters, viol players, cornet players and 'the viii musicians that follow the tent', who between them received £5 13s 4d.[37]

Naturally the official presenters of shows pronounced the royal visit a success. Churchyard was particularly impressed by the reactions of the local population. He praised 'the good order, great cheere and charges that Hir Highnesse subiects were at during hir abode in those parties' and was amazed that 'people nurtured farre from Courte should use so much courtesie'. Courtiers were welcomed by the citizens 'not with feygned ceremonies but with friendly entertaynement' and the common people who always flocked to see the Queen never had 'ynough of the sight so long wished and desired'. Everyone who came with her was pleasantly surprised by 'the rare and good maner of the peeple especially in Norwich' – in contrast to those in areas where the Queen and the Court were more often seen.

In a rather more flowery style Garter prefaced his account of the visit with a glowing description of the psychological effect of the Queen's stay in Norwich. At her arrival she 'gladded the hartes of the people there as they no lesse laboured to travayle forth to view the excellency of their soveraign'. As the week progressed, 'The Mayor, Magistrates and good Citizens employed their study and substance to holde on this happy beginning, the Prince had hir pleasures, the Nobilitie their desire, the whole trayne such intertainment as for the tyme of hir continuance there, Norwich seemed (if any such there be) a terrestriall Paradise.' Eventually came 'the frowning Friday' of her departure – but by then Garter had already gone. 'I leave', he said, 'the dolour that was to the report of them that did see it.' No wonder his book was ready to be printed by the end of the following week.

Topclyffe's letter to the Earl of Shrewsbury the following week confirmed the warmth of the Queen's reception: 'I never did see her Ma[jesty] better receved by too cuntries in one jorney then Suffolke and Norfolk now, Suffolke of gentillmen and Norfolke of the meaner sort wth excedinge joye to themselves and well-likinge to her Ma[jesty].' (His jaundiced view of the Norfolk gentry is not explained.) There had been 'great interteignment at the M[aster] of the Rowlls [Melford Hall], greater at Killinghall and exceedinge of all sorts at Norwich'.[38]

The Spanish ambassador's report to Madrid was naturally less enthusiastic. Writing a fortnight later he (or his informant) seems to have selected and heightened the news that would be welcome in Madrid. Reporting yet another version of the events at Euston, 'In the North', he said again, the Queen had met more Catholics than she expected; 'a great many images' had been found in one house and dragged round and burnt. In Norwich among the large crowds of people who came out to see her was a group of children who knelt as she passed and said, 'God Save the Queen.' She turned to them and said, 'Speak up! I know you do not love me here.'[39] If there was any truth in this little episode, Garter and Churchyard, not unnaturally, failed to mention it.

Sadly in the following months Norwich suffered a very serious outbreak of plague which lasted well into the next year. Nearly 5,000 people died, almost 150 more immigrants than natives. Understandably and perhaps with reason the infection was blamed on the progress.[40]

CHAPTER 5

PRIVATE LIVES
22 AUGUST–6 SEPTEMBER

The Recusant Hearings Begin

On Friday 22 August, when the festivities were over and the Queen was leaving Norwich, the Lords of her Council turned to the serious business of the religious resistance. During the previous year the bishops had each submitted to the Council a list of the men and women in each parish in their dioceses who refused to attend their local church as required by law. With their names was given the value of their possessions in land and goods. The Council had thus been able to draw up lists of men (only) to be examined county by county. They began with those in Norfolk and were to have others summoned by the Sheriff as they reached each county on their return journey. For Norfolk they had seventeen names out of nearly fifty submitted by the Bishop,[1] all comparatively well off. For two days they sat in Norwich with the Bishop and the two Deputy Lieutenants of the County to inquire into their cases.

On that Friday they examined six gentlemen. They came before the Council one by one and each was charged with not attending church services 'contrarie to all good lawes and orders and against the duetie of good subjects'. Each admitted the charge and then was asked if he would change and conform – that is, accept the new religion. Each refused and was sent out. When they had all been seen, the Council went through the list with the Bishop to find out whether he had previously attempted to convert any of them. It emerged that for four of them it was the first time they had been accused. These four – Humphrey Bedingfeld of Quiddenham, younger brother of Sir Henry (who was to appear later), Robert de Grey of Merton, John Downes of Boughton and John Drury of Godwick (near Tittleshall) – were called back in together and ordered to provide bail of £200 each and to stay in the houses of certain trustworthy Norwich citizens to which they had been assigned. Every day or whenever they were told, they had to meet with the Bishop or someone appointed by him to undergo instruction and persuasion until they were willing to conform. Then the Bishop had authority to release them. If they persisted in resisting his efforts until the following Michaelmas (29 September) they were to be imprisoned until they gave in – when the Bishop had to seek further orders from the Council. In fact in early October the Bishop claimed success with John Drury and released him subject to financial guarantees. His change of heart cannot have lasted, however, for some years later he and the others were again summoned, this time before the Justices of the Peace. Downes, Bedingfeld and de Grey at least continued to be listed as recusants and were fined or imprisoned for many years to come.[2]

The two others examined that day were dealt with more severely. Edward Rookwood of Euston had already been excommunicated for refusing all efforts to persuade him to conform and his Catholicism had been publicly demonstrated at his house a fortnight earlier. Robert Downes of Melton Hall had also resisted previous efforts. Both were sent to prison, to remain there without outside contact except as allowed by the Bishop either for further religious instruction or as was necessary to arrange their family affairs. Like John Drury, Rookwood was said to have conformed early in October and was released on payment of guarantees. He too returned to his faith and was still paying heavy fines for his recusancy nearly twenty years later. Robert Downes, on the other hand, though willing to listen to sermons whenever he was told to, remained obstinate in his beliefs and was to stay in prison. In October 1580 he was in Norwich prison with Humphrey Bedingfeld and the Suffolk recusants Michael Hare, Roger Martin and Edward Sulliard when he received a letter from an English Catholic in France with plans for his escape to the Continent which, although he threw it on the fire, attracted the attention of the Bishop and put them all at risk. They had to take urgent steps to assure him of their loyalty to the Queen and to protect themselves from accusations of treason.[3] Downes continued to be fined for many years and by 1602 he had lost almost all his lands, retaining only his house at Melton and its surroundings.[4]

The next day, Saturday, when the Queen had moved on to Kimberley (and one member, the Lord Chamberlain, had left for home), the Council examined another three gentlemen. Like the four of the previous day, Saturday's three were placed under house arrest in Norwich to be instructed by the Bishop. Among these was Thomas Lovell of East Harling, whose father had been an active supporter of Mary Tudor. The family had been eminent in their locality since the fifteenth century, but Thomas, anxious to sustain their position, found his political career frequently set back by allegations of recusancy – though eventually in 1601 he did achieve a knighthood.[5] Lovell's arrest did not deter the Court officials from lodging Lord Leicester, a fervent opponent of 'papistry', at his house when the progress reached Thetford the following week. Lovell was another of those 'reclaimed' by the bishop and released. He was back at home in Harling by 1 October, when he signed a letter to the Council protesting his loyalty to 'my most noble and merciful sufferen [sovereign]' and his country.[6]

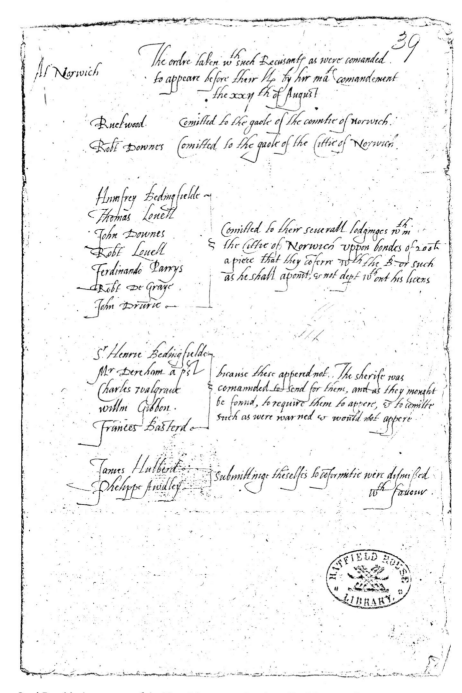

Lord Burghley's summary of the Norwich recusant hearings (Cecil Papers 161/39).

The other two seen that day, Robert Lovell of Beechamwell, Thomas's younger brother, and Ferdinand Parris from Linton, who had bought the valuable manor of Pudding Norton (south of Fakenham) only two years before,[7] continued to be suspect for many years. In 1581 Bishop Freake wrote plaintively to Parris, temporarily released, that the Council had recently complained very sharply of his leniency towards the recusants. He had therefore to urge Parris and the others to return to prison.[8] Several years later the Council again complained about the freedom of the recusants held in Norwich gaol; they 'do much harm and infect the county by the liberty which they enjoy there'. Robert Lovell and Parris, with Robert de Grey and Humphrey Bedingfeld, were to be moved to prison in Wisbech.[9]

Of the eight other gentlemen summoned before the Council, three eventually agreed to conform. 'Mr Dereham, a priest' had, as we have seen, already left Costessey. Another from Lady Jerningham's household who failed to appear was Charles Walgrave, her son-in-law, who with his wife, Hieronima, also lived at Costessey. Suspect because of his family connections and indeed a traditionalist at heart, he managed to keep within the law and the Council did not pursue him further. Another man had moved into Cambridgeshire and was already in prison there.

By Sunday 24 August the Council had caught up with the Queen and they completed their hearings of Norfolk recusants at Woodrising. Here, not far from his house at Oxborough (which had earlier been inspected by William Bowles in preparation for the progress), they examined the elderly Sir Henry Bedingfeld, who had failed to appear at Norwich. He was easily the richest of the recusants on the Bishop's list. Not surprisingly, given his age and history, he refused to conform and was sent to private lodgings in Norwich, against bail of £500. All those called before the Council were gentlemen of some substance, but here the Council also took steps against Sir Henry's servants, who were suspected of sharing their master's beliefs. They were to be examined by someone sent to Oxborough by the Bishop and if they refused to conform they were to be dismissed. Sir Henry was not to be allowed to maintain them or to take on any servants 'in any place or office about him' who were suspected of recusancy.

It was ironic – though probably not planned – that Bedingfeld should be so examined in a house where the Queen was staying. Over twenty-four years earlier, during the reign of her sister, Mary, a rebellion under Sir Thomas Wyatt led to Elizabeth's imprisonment in the Tower of London for a few weeks, followed by nearly a year of house arrest at Woodstock Palace in Oxfordshire. During that time Sir Henry Bedingfeld, a staunch supporter of Mary Tudor, was in charge of the royal prisoner. Naturally his public career ended when Elizabeth became Queen, but his troubles later in her reign were more likely due to his faith than to any personal animosity on her part.

Sir Henry Bedingfeld of Oxburgh Hall (artist unknown).

Sir Henry remained under house arrest in Norwich until early November, when the Bishop was ordered to send him to appear before the Council, now at Richmond. He set out, but by the end of the month, learning of his poor state of health from his son-in-law, Henry Sackford (the Privy Chamber officer who had delivered the Queen's gift to the immigrant communities in Norwich), the Council allowed him first to return to Norwich and then to go home. In January 1579, again on a plea from Sackford that he was too ill to travel, he was given leave to stay there until Lady Day, when he was again due to travel to Richmond. This concession, said the Council, was a favour which was not to be abused. In fact he stayed at home for over two years until the death of his wife. Sackford then sought and obtained the Council's permission for him to go to his daughter's house at Wiggenhall St Mary in the Norfolk fens to recover from his loss and to stay, they said, 'intil he maie passe over the remembraunce of the ladie his wyfe'. He himself died the following year.

The last man to be examined at this time was also summoned to Woodrising. Edmund Wyndham, an illegitimate son of Sir Edmund Wyndham of Felbrigg, had been Professor of Civil Law at Cambridge but had lost his post in 1559 when he refused to acknowledge Elizabeth as head of the Church. He was not on the Bishop's list of recusants or Burghley's list of Norfolk gentlemen. He may not have been resident in the county, but perhaps being found there was added to the Council's list. Like Sir Henry, he refused to conform and was placed in lodgings in Norwich on payment of £200. He was still obdurate in September and the Council ordered him to attend them at Richmond since 'no mylde course will serve to reforme him'. His half-brother Francis Wyndham, Recorder of Norwich, Sergeant at Law and respected London lawyer, undertook to ensure that he did so. By 1580 he was living in Paris but soon returned and was imprisoned at Wisbech. Eventually he signed a letter vowing loyalty to the Queen and was released.[10]

Naturally the professional persecutor of recusants, Topclyffe, was delighted by the Council's moves. His dramatic account of events at Euston has already been given. In the same letter on 30 August he reported the imprisonment of 'yonge Rookwoode' and Robert Downes and that seven others had been 'comytted to severall houses in Norwych as presoners'. He made no mention of those who were heard at Woodrising or later; evidently his only sources of information were his contacts in Norwich while he was there. On the other hand, he said, a number of Puritan preachers who had been silenced by the Bishop had now been allowed to resume, giving 'a greater and more universall joye to the cuntrees and the moste of the Coort than the disgraice of the Papists'.[11]

In fact, the Council had made a major and public stand on the middle ground between the extremes of Catholicism and Puritanism and Bishop Freake had been shown the way he was expected to go. He had been appointed in 1575 to suppress Puritanism, which his predecessor had not sufficiently discouraged. This he had done with vigour but had provoked such strong reactions from powerful local men that, following the Council's visit, he had to moderate his policies. He had also seemed to lean too far in the other direction and to show leniency to the Catholics. His letter to Ferdinand Parris already mentioned certainly sounds sympathetic. Indeed, one of a series of reports on his dispute with his Chancellor mentions a known recusant called Downes (probably Robert) as saying that the Bishop was 'on our side'. The same source also provided a scrap of local gossip about the Bishop. It was well known throughout all Norfolk, it said, that 'whatsoever Mrs Freake will have done the Bishop must and will accomplyse'[12] – he seems to have had something in common with Trollope's Bishop Proudie.

Altogether Freake had an uncomfortable time in Norwich and five years later he asked to be moved from 'that troublesome and unquiet place' where he had suffered 'continual crossing and overthwarting to my great grief and unquietness'.[13] Eventually in 1584 he moved to Worcester, but not before Norwich was refused by one possible replacement because of 'the troblesomnes and the dainger of the diocesse'.[14]

Across Norfolk

The Queen left Norwich in the late afternoon of Friday 22 August. Among her entourage was, as usual, Lord Sussex, her Lord Chamberlain. He rode as far as the city boundary, keeping an eye on the proceedings, as we have seen, but now that the official entertainments were over, he had permission to leave the Court and at Earlham Bridge he set off for home. He had been authorized earlier to hire seven carts to carry back to London the luggage which he had brought with him on the progress; four could then go on to Bath, where he was taking his wife, the former Frances Sidney, Sir Philip's aunt, for treatment. He was at home in Bermondsey by the beginning of the next week and on Thursday 28 August he wrote to the Queen with an account of his conversation with the French envoy M. de Quissé, who had called on him about seven o'clock on the previous Tuesday morning on his way back to Court from the Netherlands.[15] The following day, in spite of a 'flux' he had caught on the way home, he and Frances set off to Bath, 'where', he said, 'God give her that comfort she hopes for'. By mid-September she had both taken the water and gone into the bath but 'the stone she brought with her' was no better. He himself was passing the time attending her and making 'good cheer' with the friends he had found there. Whether or not she was helped by her visit to Bath, Frances outlived her husband and died in 1589, leaving £5,000 to found Sidney Sussex College in Cambridge.

As she moved on, the Queen's retinue must have been noticeably reduced without Lord Sussex and the seven other councillors (and their servants and followers) who stayed behind to hear, on the Saturday, the last three recusants who had been summoned to Norwich.

Elizabeth's next lodging place, which she reached late on the Friday evening, was the fortified and moated Kimberley Tower, built at the beginning of the previous century by Sir John Wodehouse. Her host was Roger Wodehouse, a descendant of the builder of the house which he had inherited at the age of twenty from his grandfather. When the Queen came he was thirty-seven, one of an old and eminent Norfolk family. He was a magistrate and later an MP. Although in religion his inclinations were towards the traditional and against the extremes of Puritanism – witness his friendship with Philip, Earl of Surrey, who was godfather to his son and had a room kept for him at Kimberley – he managed to display an acceptable Protestantism and kept within the law.[16] His knighthood a few days later recognized his value to the government in his county and perhaps was intended also to encourage such conformity.

When the Queen came, the house had over twenty rooms of various sizes for living and sleeping, as well as the kitchen, armoury, brewhouse, granary and stables.[17] (Part had collapsed by 1623 and in 1659 it was demolished; later a new house was built on a different site.) Curiously, the house was not on William Bowles's list to be surveyed, but Symon Bowyer and his team who were not used at Norwich had plenty of time to move on from Bracon Ash. Raphe Hope came direct from Norwich for his two days. According to Churchyard, who travelled with the progress for some of the way back, she was 'well receyved and nobly entertayned' there.

While the Queen stayed at Kimberley, some of the Court were as usual lodged elsewhere. The Earl of Leicester, arriving from Norwich the day after the Queen, stayed at Downham Lodge, less than 2 miles away.[18] The house had originally been built by the Abbot of Wymondham Abbey and had passed through several hands before it was bought by William Thornton in 1564 or 1565. Leicester's host nearly fourteen years later was Oliver Thornton, a minor landowner who would have had no choice in opening his house to so eminent a guest. Early in the following century it was acquired by the Wodehouse family, who lived there until they built their new house in the eighteenth century.[19]

Elizabeth's visit to Kimberley was clearly a formal occasion and a great throne had been erected for her there. Like the one in Norwich Cathedral, it was hung with crimson velvet. It had panels embroidered with the arms of Roger Wodehouse and Mary Corbet, his wife,[20] and seems to have been created by Symon Bowyer from some of the fine velvet already in use in the house. The inventory of its contents made on Sir Roger's death ten years later makes no mention of a throne but the bed in the Great Chamber had a canopy of crimson velvet decorated with the arms of Sir Roger, as well as six double silk curtains and a red velvet valance fringed with red silk. The cushions in the two windowseats were of red satin embroidered with silver and gold and red velvet. The Earl of Surrey's room at Kimberley matched his own at Kenninghall in luxury. It also had bed hangings of red velvet and gold and cushions

The Kimberley throne, reconstructed at the Burrell Collection as for the Queen's visit.

of worked red velvet. Another bedchamber was decorated in tawny and orange and Lady Wodehouse's was mainly red and blue. The usher and his team had plenty of rich furnishings to choose from in preparing the Queen's suite of rooms. One room was still called the 'Quene's Chamber' in 1588.

The throne, apparently reconstructed later, survived at Kimberley until the present century, when it came to the Burrell Collection in Glasgow. A bodice and a pair of sleeves, said to have been left by the Queen, were also in the possession of the Wodehouse family at Kimberley until the nineteenth century.

There was also at Kimberley, until at least the nineteenth century, another valance which if she saw it must have held poignant associations for Elizabeth. It was decorated with the letters HA entwined and the emblems of Henry VIII and her ill-fated mother, Anne Boleyn.[21] It had probably come to Kimberley through the family's links with the Boleyns of Blickling, less than 20 miles to the north (later the home of Edward Clere). Roger Wodehouse's mother was Raphe Shelton's sister and, as we have seen in connection with Raphe's knighthood, their grandmother had been another Anne Boleyn.

Curiously, it was another Wodehouse, not directly related, who was knighted at Kimberley. This was Henry Wodehouse of Waxham,[22] who was a good deal more radical in religion than Roger. He too was important in local administration, holding office as a magistrate with hardly a break for nearly forty years and twice being an MP. He lived to the considerable age of seventy-eight.

Another Norfolk man, eminent in a rather wider sphere, was knighted at the same time. Thomas Gawdy came from Claxton, a few miles south-east of Norwich, where he too had an old fortified and moated house. He had also built a new house, Gawdy Hall, at Redenhall, on the Norfolk–Suffolk border, which, unlike Kimberley, had been inspected by William Bowles. He came from a family of successful lawyers and landowners and had himself acquired considerable property through purchase and two rich marriages. He had been a magistrate and an MP, but his career lay in the law and by 1574 he had become a Judge of the Queen's Bench.[23] His religious respectability was clearly unquestioned.

Once again John North made a brief appearance at Court. He and his father had reached home the day before and Lord North was evidently now to stay at Kirtling, supervising the tremendous preparations for the Queen's arrival. On Saturday 23 August, however, he sent John back to Kimberley, presumably with some message or inquiry. He evidently needed an early reply, for John returned to Kirtling the same night. The long round trip cost him 5s for the horses and a midday meal at Thetford. From then on he too stayed at home until the Queen came.[24]

On Sunday 24 August the Queen moved on the 5 or 6 miles to Woodrising Hall, the home of the Southwell family. William Bowles had visited it earlier and a new team spent six days there organizing the Queen's apartments. This was the group under Gentleman Usher Piers Pennante which at the outset of the progress had come no further than Alderman Branch's house at Theydon Garnon but now joined the two others. Charles Smythe from the Wardrobe, who had attended the Queen when she went hunting at Costessey on the previous Tuesday, spent four days at Woodrising. Churchyard was not at this stopping place and evidently failed to find out what happened there, 'wherefore', he said rather unfairly, 'I give it no greate commendation'.

As usual the Purveyors had organized supplies from the local communities. According to tradition, a farm at the nearby village of Letton sent butter and milk to Woodrising while the Queen was there. The manor of Shipdham, 3 or 4 miles to the north, contributed wax for the document seals costing 8s 0d, wheat at 10s 8d and oats for the horses at 4s 6d. They also rang the church bells 'at the Quenes beyng here'; the ringers were paid eight pennyworth of bread and drink.[25] If indeed Elizabeth visited Shipdham, rather than being within earshot of the bells, it must have been on Monday 25 August and she probably went hunting in the deer park owned by the Waxham branch of the Wodehouse family, one of whom she had just knighted.

The Southwells had been another important Norfolk family, the brothers Richard and Robert having held high office under Henry VIII. Sir Richard was also a member of the Privy Council under both Edward VI and Mary Tudor, but when Elizabeth became Queen he was suspected of loyalty to the old faith and he lost his position both nationally and in his county. When he died in 1564, he left no legitimate heir, the children of his second wife having been born before he married her. His brother Robert had died earlier, in 1559, and his estate went to Robert's son Thomas. He died a few years later and it was therefore to his son Robert's house the Queen came in 1578. He, however, was still a minor, only fifteen, and could not yet inherit, so the hall was held by his stepmother, his father's third wife. She, Nazaret, had remarried after Thomas Southwell's death and was now Lady Paget.[26] As with the other minor owners of houses selected for their convenience on the royal route, she probably had little to do with the arrangements.

At this time the family was living in comparative obscurity, with the heir still a boy and a background of recusancy. Indeed, Nazaret's husband, Lord Paget, was a known Catholic who, two years later, provided the venue in Smithfield for a sermon by the Jesuit priest Robert Campion[27] and was himself imprisoned for his faith. In 1583 he fled to Paris, to cure his gout and satisfy his conscience, as he said in a letter to Lord Burghley. Lord Paget cannot have been at Woodrising at this time and was probably already living apart from his wife. As early as 1573 Gilbert Talbot described him as 'an evell husband' who would not allow his wife to keep any of her former, Southwell, servants.[28] Their separation was formalized in 1581–2. The Council's arrival in the house and their examination of two recusants there, as already described, must have caused some anxiety, but they evidently saw no threat from what remained of the Southwell family and no harm came to them.

In time young Robert was to reverse the family fortunes entirely. In the spring of 1583, aged twenty, he married Elizabeth, the daughter of Lord Howard of Effingham, the Queen's long-serving loyal servant, successor to Lord Sussex as Lord Chamberlain in 1584 and, the following year, Lord Admiral of England. The Queen attended the wedding. Two years later Robert was knighted and made Vice-Admiral of Norfolk[29] and in 1588, still only twenty-five, he commanded the *Elizabeth Jonas*, the third-largest (at 900 tons) and one of the oldest ships in action against the Armada. (As early as 1559 the Queen had been at a banquet held on board while the ship was moored off Woolwich.) Robert died only ten years later, eminent both nationally and locally, and was buried magnificently in Woodrising Church. Near his tomb is a brass plate recording the death of his first son, aged three.

Sir Robert's daughter Elizabeth achieved short-lived notoriety when in 1605, still in her teens, she eloped with Lord Leicester's illegitimate son, yet another Robert. He was the son of Douglas, Lady Sheffield, who had been Leicester's mistress in the early 1570s. His father had refused to marry Douglas, insisting, with reason, that the Queen's reaction would spell disaster. He did, however, acknowledge his son and bring him up from the age of ten. In 1605, long after his father's death, Robert, now over thirty, tried to legalize his position and claimed his father's title and property. When he failed, he left England for ever, taking with him, although he was still married to his second wife, Elizabeth Southwell disguised as a page – and providing James I with an opportunity to take over Lord Leicester's estates. Eventually they settled in Florence, where he became a shipbuilder and engineer – and father of thirteen children, having turned Catholic and married their mother by papal dispensation. His Puritan father would have been very grieved.

At Woodrising on the Sunday, as we have seen, the remaining seven members of the Council examined the last two Norfolk recusants. They also had time to deal with several other items of business, not all of them local. They were still concerned about a dispute which had arisen the previous year in Dover over the election of the Mayor and they sent for the town's charter; they ordered two Norfolk lawyers to examine a personal complaint against the Bishop of Norwich and either settle it themselves or submit the details for decision by the Council; several Norfolk dignitaries were similarly either to settle a claim by a Dutch citizen against a local man or to send the defendant to the Council with a report on the facts; and they arranged for a Southampton merchant to be protected from his creditors and for a Yarmouth man to be released from prison on bail.

On Tuesday 26 August the Queen set off on one of the longest stages of the progress, nearly 15 miles to Thetford. She left early in the morning and reached Breckles Hall, about half-way, for dinner. Usher Piers Pennante had managed to combine his six days at Woodrising with arranging 'a dyninge howse' there. The Wardrobe man in attendance was Raphe Hope, who came on from Kimberley to spend the day.

Breckles Hall had been built by Francis Wodehouse, second cousin to Roger of Kimberley. Francis's second wife, Eleanor, was a known recusant and in 1601 she was excommunicated.[30] Her husband also accepted her faith, probably later in life and after the visit of the Queen and Council; certainly no action was taken against them at this time, though by the end of the century he had had to sell his fine new house.[31] Like others whose houses were used in this way, he probably had little to do with the Queen's dinner except to hand over the hall to the Court servants. This was a routine occasion with no feasting or entertainment; it held no interest for Churchyard and he made no mention of this or any other similar dinner stops on the way back.

In the afternoon the long procession continued its journey to Thetford, its last stopping place in Norfolk. In the Middle Ages Thetford had been an important ecclesiastical centre, with five religious houses, twenty churches and several monastic hospitals. Its economy had begun to decline early in the sixteenth century, but after the Dissolution of the Monasteries its revenue from the religious institutions and the pilgrims they attracted had disappeared and its importance and wealth were much diminished. Already in 1539 the Mayor complained that the pilgrims were 'abhorryd

Breckles Hall, Norfolk home of Francis Wodehouse.

exesepulsyd and sette apart forever wherby a grett nombyr of peopyll . . . by idyllyd and lyke to be browght ynto extreme beggarye'.[32] It had, however, after considerable and lengthy efforts, obtained a royal charter in 1574 and was now governed independently of the Crown by a formally constituted corporation.

The Corporation had known of the Queen's coming since mid-June and had made their preparations, much like Norwich's but on a minor scale: 'bridgegate strete', through which she would enter the town, was repaired and the citizens were instructed to clean up not only their houses but also the roadways in front of them.

In readiness for the official reception, the Mayor's sword of office was renovated and given a new scabbard. One of the two maces had been 'lost', apparently by the previous Mayor, John Shering, and the other, which also needed some repairs, was taken to Bury St Edmunds to be copied, Mr Shering bearing the cost. To help with the town's expenses John Reynolds, the Recorder (the permanent legal officer to the Corporation) lent them £40 in gold with an offer of as much again if necessary, all to be repaid by Michaelmas, 29 September.

All the ten present burgesses and their predecessors had to provide themselves with red gowns and the twenty members of the Corporation who were commoners had to have 'decent apparell'; woe betide anyone who failed in this. Indeed on 26 July one man was fined 12d for appearing at a meeting without his gown. The Mayor was taking no chances and the whole company was ordered to attend on 6 August 'in suche decent apparell as they will use at the Quene's Maiestie's cominge'; even so two burgesses and four commoners failed to appear, although display of their gowns was the only purpose of the assembly. Concern for their costumes may explain a special authority issued on 21 June for drapers and others from outside the town to come in to Thetford market.

Thetford Corporation included some very argumentative and difficult burgesses. Their meeting on 16 August, for example, the day the Queen reached Norwich, was called specifically to decide on 'the better provision of all thinges to be sett in good order for their duetifull receyvinge of her maiestie', but their discussions were so disrupted by Richard Evance and Thomas Allyn that nothing could be settled. Resentful of being called to order, both announced, rashly, that they no longer wished to remain on the Corporation – and were taken at their word. Immediately they 'were dismissed of their burgisship' and two others chosen. Not that the disruptive pair went quietly; Mr Evance was heard to say that he would 'pull him out by the eares' if anyone replaced him. To avoid further trouble at the guildhall, the two new burgesses were sworn in at the Recorder's house.

Eventually all was ready and the Queen arrived in the late afternoon or early evening of Tuesday 26 August. As at Norwich, she would have been met at the town boundary by the Mayor, Peter Scott, preceded by his sword-bearer and accompanied by his two sergeants, carrying the maces, and the Corporation in their new or refurbished gowns. As usual – and expected – the Queen was presented with a gift, a silver-gilt covered cup weighing 16¾ oz (rather lightweight compared with some earlier donations).

Elizabeth also received, possibly with the cup, a 'supplication' (subject unknown) presented by the Mayor and Corporation. No answer had arrived by the following January and they asked Recorder Reynolds to take up the matter with the Council.[33] Evidently he was successful, for he was later granted 20s for 'getting of answer of a supplication exhibited to the Queen's Majestie in the Progresse in Norfolk'.[34]

The now inflated procession made its way to a house belonging to the newly knighted Sir Edward Clere on the southern outskirts of the town. Clere lived at Blickling, the great mansion some 12 miles north of Norwich, but he had acquired the buildings and lands of the former nunnery of St George through his wife, Frances. Her father, Sir Richard Fulmerston, had been granted them, and much else, in 1539 at the dissolution of several Thetford religious houses and had made his home in the nunnery. When he died, in 1567, his property went to his daughter and her husband, who made certain alterations to the house and added some rooms.

There was also in Thetford a house which had belonged to the executed Duke of Norfolk. At the time of his death six years earlier, it had been richly furnished,[35] but in 1578 the Court officers chose not to use another Howard house, at least for the Queen herself. Perhaps it was not big enough, having only a dozen or so rooms for living and sleeping, or perhaps it had been emptied and not used for some years – though the Howard agent, Thomas Heyward, was still in Thetford in 1578. William Bowles had come on his surveying trip but which house or houses he inspected is not recorded. For whatever reason, it was Edward Clere's house that was prepared for the Queen by Anthony Wingfeld, who had last been working in Norwich, and by Raphe Hope, who came on from Kimberley and, like Charles Smythe at Woodrising, stayed for four days.

The entertainments by Clere and the Norfolk gentry assembled to see Elizabeth off were doubtless lavish. Churchyard, who did not get to Thetford, was still able to find out from those who did that they were 'worthily feasted'. Sir Nicholas Lestrange, and probably others, had not stayed with the progress for the whole of its route in Norfolk but they reassembled for the Queen's last stop in their county. Lestrange had ridden direct to Thetford from Norwich and arrived a day before Elizabeth. He stayed in Thetford, but again some of his horses had to be stabled at West Harling.[36] The Howard house may well have been used to accommodate some of the gentlemen and officials, probably including Lestrange, but it was not considered suitable for Lord Leicester. He went to East Harling, the home of Thomas Lovell,[37] although, as we have seen, his host was still under house arrest in Norwich.

The following day, Wednesday 27 August, the Council held a meeting attended by the seven faithful members who had been with the progress almost all of the time.

Among other business, they were now able to consider the complaints about their neighbours that Lord Burghley and Lord Leicester had heard from the Bailiffs of Yarmouth during their short visit there while the Queen was in Norwich. The Yarmouth men must have thought the cost of the visit well spent when they heard that the Council had banned fish markets and the selling of 'any herringes or fish' in certain neighbouring villages.

The Council also heard some minor personal disputes between yet more troublesome Thetford personalities. In April the Corporation had heard evidence that one John Palferye had called a Mr Medcalfe 'knave and stinckinge knave' and they had put him in prison. Mr Medcalfe, evidently still incensed, seized his opportunity in August to complain to the Council, who, understandably, told the Mayor and Recorder to deal with him. Two days later Palferye and another man who had also offended Mr Medcalfe were summoned before the Mayor; both admitted their guilt and were sent back to prison.

There was also the Corporation's case against Mr William Davye, who had been Mayor in 1576 and was accused of fraud during his year as Coroner in 1577. He was a bitter opponent of the Recorder and principal cause of controversy in the town. Their lordships ordered that 'for the better and more quiet government' of the town, he should be deprived of his status as burgess and their decision was formally adopted at a meeting of the Corporation on 29 August. Some time later, however, Davye managed to regain his position and to remove the Recorder and his deputy, the town clerk, from their posts. When in December 1581 Recorder Reynolds complained to the Council about his treatment in Thetford, they wrote severely to the Mayor and burgesses, commanding them to reinstate their original officers and to reimpose 'the reasonable quietness' in which the Council had left the town at their departure from Mr Clere's house three years earlier. The Mayor and William Davye were to report to the Council forthwith so that 'this whole cause' could be fully considered. They arrived on 18 December, but the Council had no time to deal with so minor a matter and eventually it was referred to a group of local commissioners. They reported in August 1582 on their attempts to settle the disputes in Thetford, calling William Davye 'the chief author of all factions'. In spite of all efforts, controversy continued in the town for several years more.

It was not until that same Wednesday in Thetford that the Queen knighted Roger Wodehouse, although he had been her host at Kimberley the previous weekend. He must have come with the progress from there and may well have been among the Norfolk gentlemen who accompanied the Queen across their county. Her official duty done, however, the Queen did not linger; perhaps, though Clere was a rich man, his in-laws' house was not to her liking. Unexpectedly – her officials had prepared for at least a two-night stay – Elizabeth moved on the same day. Her journey was comparatively short and she probably left after dinner. The Norfolk gentlemen were free to return to their homes, somewhat poorer than they had set out. Attending the Queen had cost Sir Nicholas Lestrange £24 4s 8d.

The town, on the other hand, had only spent £16 2s ½d: a high proportion, £6 14s 8d, in payments to the royal servants; £6 7s 6d for the cup; and £2 19s 10½d on the regalia – this at least was an investment. The following week, mindful of the need to repay the Recorder's loan by the end of September, the Mayor called a meeting to ask for voluntary contributions towards the cost of the Queen's visit. Six burgesses and ten commoners paid up, offering varying amounts from 10s to 2d. Naturally the three deprived of their seats were not among them, though they were better off than many of their colleagues; the outspoken Mr Evance was recorded as flatly refusing to give anything. In all the Mayor was able to collect only £2 7s 10d.[38] Clearly the Queen was leaving an impoverished town.

At Hengrave Hall

By the evening of Wednesday 27 August the Queen had reached Hengrave Hall, the large and handsome house of Sir Thomas Kytson, whom she had knighted on her way north. Thomas Kytson senior had been a wealthy London merchant who bought the manor of Hengrave in 1521 and four years later began building his great house. It took him thirteen years, so towards the end of that time he was able to acquire and use building material from some of the dissolved local monasteries. He also enlarged his fortune by buying some of the lands of the former St Edmund's Abbey. One of his daughters married Sir William Spring, the Sheriff who was probably escorting the Queen again now that she was back in Suffolk.

Thomas senior died in 1540, leaving his widow, Margaret, to give birth to his son and heir. She later married John Bouchier, Earl of Bath, a supporter of Mary Tudor, who is said to have come to Hengrave on the death of Edward VI in 1553 en route to Kenninghall. Bouchier accompanied her and joined her followers there. Young Thomas thus grew up in a Catholic household. In his teens he married Jane Paget, sister of Thomas, the disagreeable Catholic husband of Nazaret Southwell. She died when he was still only eighteen and within two years he married Elizabeth Cornwallis, whose father had been in the service of the Duke of Norfolk at Kenninghall and had held office under Queen Mary herself. Under Elizabeth, such a conservative background made Thomas suspected of adherence to the old ways and at the fall of the Duke of Norfolk he was implicated by association and imprisoned. To save himself, he wrote urgently to the Queen, protesting his loyalty and offering to serve her in any way he could 'while my life and breath remain'. He had realized that his replies to the Council's questions about his religious practices had been less than convincing and he was now anxious to reaffirm his strict adherence to the Protestant faith; henceforth he and his family would attend church as required and he himself

The Queen's host at Hengrave, Sir Thomas Kytson (George Gower, 1573).

Sir Thomas Kytson's second wife Elizabeth (George Gower, 1573).

would make more effort to hear sermons and 'the persuasions of wise and learned men'. His declaration was evidently accepted and his willingness to conform was later rewarded with the knighthood granted at Bury St Edmunds. Nevertheless, he remained a traditionalist and even ten years later he and his wife were suspected of recusancy.

At Hengrave and at his house in the City of London, Thomas maintained a lavish and cultured lifestyle. The Queen's new lodging place must have been much more to her liking, and that of her entourage, than the converted nunnery she had just left. It had over fifty rooms for living and sleeping, richly appointed and furnished. As in other great houses, the plain glass of the windows was enlivened by coloured glass shields with the family's arms. Each family member had a pair of rooms, an outer and an inner chamber. One room in the master suite was still called the Queen's chamber when Sir Thomas died over twenty years later. Others were allocated to his wife, to his mother (even long after she had died) and to his father-in-law. The family's rooms included 'the painted chamber', a summer and a winter parlour, and 'the bathing chamber' close to the nursery and to Lady Kytson's rooms. Officers of the household such as the clerk of the kitchen, the bailiff and the yeoman, and servants like the nursery maid, the dairy maid, the gardener, the thatcher and the brewer, had a room each. Specialist areas included the armoury, the wardrobe, the linen room, the laundry, the kitchen and the wine cellar. There were places for making and storing the candles, cheese, beer and fish. This vast and complex estate had been highly esteemed by Thomas's mother. When she married the Earl of Bath, her marriage settlement stipulated that he should live at Hengrave 'forasmuch as the dwelling . . . is very commodious, profitable, necessary and delectable for the health, wealth and pleasure of the earl'.

Sir Thomas's will in 1602 left £5 each to every poor person in Bury St Edmunds and in ten nearby villages; 40s each to his household servants, mentioning particularly 'John Grey the poor fellow in the kitchen'; and the large sum of £20 to Thomas Cassel, a lad who served in his bedchamber. He also remembered with regret that he had engineered the marriage of his wife's sister, Mary Cornwallis, to his nephew the young Earl of Bath, who had inherited the title from his grandfather. Mary's marriage had proved 'most unfortunate and to her great hindrance' and Thomas left her £300 in recognition of the great trouble he had caused her. The residue of his estate went to his widow, who kept up the grand Hengrave style for over twenty-five years.[39]

After Thomas's death the name of Kytson disappeared from Hengrave. He left only two daughters – his one son died in infancy – and his father's other four children were all girls. Indeed, of his mother's eleven children by her three husbands only two were boys.[40]

Hengrave had not been on William Bowles's tour of inspection but the sketch map of the route Elizabeth was expected to take between Thetford and Harrow (see Chapter 1) showed Hengrave as the next stopping place.

Preparations for the Queen's arrival had been made by Usher Symon Bowyer and his team moving on after finishing at Woodrising. The house was richly furnished and they can have had no difficulty in creating a range of suitable rooms. They also spent two days, as they had at Melford Hall, setting up a banqueting house in readiness for some special entertainment. Surprisingly, no Wardrobe officer is recorded; probably some of Raphe Hope's apparently wasted four days at Thetford were spent at Hengrave.

Certainly the hospitality was generous and elaborate. Churchyard, who was there, judged 'the fare and banquets' as far exceeding those at a number of other places (which he did not name). A show was put on featuring fairies – not of his devising but, he conceded, it was 'as well as might be'. During the entertainment the Queen was presented with 'a rich jewell', a gift from her host. There would have been plenty of music which she would have enjoyed. The house had a music room and certainly in 1602 there were over forty instruments and more than fifty books of music. A musician, Robert Johnson, was a member of the household in the 1570s and later in the century John Wilby, the madrigalist, lived there.[41]

Elizabeth stayed for three nights at Hengrave, where the Council had a busy schedule. They met three times, all seven councillors attending, and turned their attention once more to the Catholic threat. As they had at Norwich, they interviewed a group of suspected recusants chosen from a list of thirty-four names.[42] This time the Bishop was not present and the Council sent back to him the results of their deliberations. Nine had been sentenced. Henry Drury, in whose house the Queen had dined on her way to Bury St Edmunds, and two others, Michael Hare of Bruisyard, the son of Mary Tudor's Master of the Rolls, and Roger Martin of Melford, refused to conform and were to be imprisoned in Ipswich. Another staunch Catholic, John Daniel of Acton, was similarly due to be imprisoned in Bury. In practice, however, they were confined not in prison, but in the houses of certain reliable citizens, subject to religious argument and persuasion until Michaelmas. Of the five others, four, including Edmund Bedingfeld of Denham (son of Sir Henry), whose marriage two years before had been illegally celebrated according to the old rites,[43] and Henry Everard of Linstead, were allocated to houses in Bury and one, Edward Sulliard, went to Ipswich. A tenth man agreed to conform and was ordered to provide the Bishop with certificates to prove that he was indeed attending church as required. All the others were to remain indefinitely under house arrest or in (or were threatened with) prison. An incident in 1580 when Hare, Martin and Sulliard were in Norwich prison with Robert Downes has already been described.

The Council, however, was neither totally consistent nor intransigent. Their policy was to convert all resistance to a moderate form of Protestantism and to protect the country from the threat of Catholicism and the influence of Spain. The fines and financial bonds put up by the recusants must have been useful to the Crown and they did not wish any serious physical harm to those whose only crime lay in their beliefs.

Edmund Bedingfeld, for example, was a sick man. In November they agreed that for the sake of his health he could move to Leiston Abbey near the Suffolk coast, provided that the Bishop sent 'some learned preacher' to induce him to conform. In May of the following year he was released on bail to take the waters at Bath until the following Michaelmas, when he was to return to confinement as decided by the Bishop. He evidently did so, in improved health, for in February 1580 he was again released, this time to look after his affairs until the end of the Easter term, and this remission was extended in May so that he could arrange the legal processes of his son's marriage to the daughter of Henry Jerningham.

The Council were also willing to take account of the plague. In the summer of 1579 an outbreak occurred in Bury and Henry Drury, Thomas Sulliard, brother of Edward, and John Daniel, all now in prison, were removed to private houses where the risk of infection was reduced. Henry Everard, also in prison, was actually released in August that year after pleas on behalf of his dying wife and their fourteen children by her brother, Bassingbourne Gaudy, an eminent Norfolk politician. He and his brother-in-law had to deposit £200 between them to ensure that he would return to confinement whenever he was summoned. Catherine Everard's health improved a little after a visit by her brother just before her husband's release but, said one of her daughters, her doctor saw no hope of her recovery.[44]

As a wider move against the Catholic threat, the Council issued orders from Hengrave to sheriffs and magistrates throughout the country to arrest certain 'Popish prestes' who were travelling in disguise.

By now the Queen was regretting having offered any practical help to the Dutch and on 29 August she issued a long formal letter to the ambassadors in the Low Countries, setting out the conditions under which she might feel able to help them with money. Several individuals also took advantage of the dispatch of mail to Antwerp to write private letters to Walsingham. Burghley, Leicester and Wilson all commented on the contents of the Queen's letter, her unwillingness either to offer direct help to the Dutch on the one hand or, on the other, to encourage the Duc d'Alençon's suit and so assist them indirectly. All three sounded frustrated and depressed by the Queen's inaction. Burghley could only urge patience: 'you must perforce bear with the same as we do, that is to behold miseries coming and to be denied remedies'. Leicester was equally pessimistic: 'what good can follow, I little look for any'.

Sir Thomas Heneage, who was not a councillor, also wrote to Walsingham. He too sounded discouraged, saying, 'yf we prosper yt must be as our custome is, by miracle', and sour about the fawning ways of the Court – a man 'ys not a courtier vi dayes but can lerne how to make hym self acceptable'. On the other hand, he applauded the Council's anti-recusant measures. They have, he said, 'most consyderately straytened dyvers obstinate and arche papystes that would not coome to the churche' and the Puritan preachers' position had been restored. Although 'the foolysh Bisshoppe' had complained to the Queen about certain gentlemen of Norfolk and Suffolk as 'favorers of . . . purytanes' and 'hynderers of her proceedynges', during this progress she had come to see them as 'zealous and loyall gentlemen'.[45]

A more private and confidential letter to Walsingham was written by his own man, Edmund Tremayne. His letter reflects clearly the problems of the less important officials on a progress. He was evidently not always accommodated near his seniors and complained that he spent half the day riding to and from the Court and the rest hardly more profitably in places where it was difficult to write. His letter was finished 'stealing time as I can get it by fits'.

In it Tremayne, writing discreetly but in a direct and lively manner, described two conversations he had had with 'the gentleman you appointed me to', meaning Sir Christopher Hatton. Acting for his real master, he had flattered Hatton and then asked him how the Queen had reacted to Walsingham's latest report. Hatton had replied cryptically and Tremayne had not dared to question him further. On the subject of help for the Dutch, however, Hatton had said, 'By my troth, she is ever loth to lay out money.' Tremayne had later used the dispatch of these letters as an excuse to ask Hatton if he had any message for Walsingham and to try to discover more about the Queen's opinion of him. She was, said Hatton, very well satisfied and Tremayne could tell him so. Nevertheless, Tremayne thought Hatton less well informed than he might be about affairs in the Netherlands and suggested that his master might write in some detail to 'your friend to whom you committed me'; his letter should appear spontaneous, sent without prompting from Tremayne.

All these letters were to be carried by John Sommers, 'one of the Clarkes of Her Maiestie's Signett' – that is, a member of the office which held the Queen's private seal and a person of some importance. He had arrived from the Netherlands to find the Court at Norwich on Thursday 21 August and had come on with them to Hengrave. He was a trusted official who was expected by Secretary Wilson to add verbally to what he had written: to the ambassadors, Wilson said, 'For this matrimonial conference I know not what to write. Let Mr Sommers say his knowledge to you.' Sommers's understanding of policy was also recognized by Heneage: 'For all matters concerning your negotiation there I refer you to Mr Sommers who understands them better than myself.' Sommers left on 29 August. By 2 September Walsingham had read the Queen's letter and was writing back to Burghley.

Across Cambridgeshire

The following day, Saturday 30 August, Elizabeth turned westward to her next stopping place, Chippenham in Cambridgeshire. This was another place not inspected by Bowles but the later sketch map showed it as 8 miles from Hengrave. She probably had the morning meal at Hengrave and left in the early afternoon, arriving in time for supper at the house of Thomas Revet. Usher Piers Pennante had come on ahead from Woodrising and Breckles, and Raphe Hope came from Thetford (or Hengrave) for three days' work on the Wardrobe.

Thomas Revet was another wealthy London merchant, a mercer turned landowner. He came of a Stowmarket family, his father, also Thomas, having owned several manors in that area. His elder brother, James, had inherited their father's estates and two of his local parishes sent over some supplies for the Queen's visit: a calf, some butter, 'capons, cockrels and pulletts'. Thomas was the second son and had made his fortune in the City of London, where he had a house, but in 1572, aged fifty-three, he had bought the manor of Chippenham, where he lived till his death ten years later.[46]

Like Thomas Kytson, he was a conservative at heart and took no part in national politics. He married twice and had three daughters by his first wife (one of whom died 'in her cradel') and one by the second. This later marriage reflected his natural inclinations towards the old religion, for Griselda was another sister of the Catholic Thomas, Lord Paget. She was the seventh Paget daughter and must have been younger than Jane, Kytson's first wife, who died in 1558. Her own daughter, Anne, was born in 1568. Revet kept in touch with his Catholic in-laws but he was able to conform to the required Protestantism sufficiently not to lose favour with the Council. Indeed, in 1580 he was knighted at Westminster.[47]

When in October 1582 Revet was known to be dying, Lord North (a neighbour and the Queen's next host) wrote to Lord Burghley, knowing that on their father's death he would become the guardian of Revet's two unmarried daughters. North, who was by then, at fifty-two, a widower, had in mind marriage with the elder, Alice, aged eighteen, who would be very well endowed. He also suggested that the younger, Anne, now fourteen, who would herself inherit a considerable income, would be a good match for one of Burghley's grandsons, the children of his elder son, Sir Thomas Cecil (the eldest of Thomas's several sons was then seventeen). Revet had already disposed of his lands, bestowing upon Anne all his manors in Suffolk and the manor of Osleworth in Gloucestershire, which he had bought from Sir Nicholas Poinz, coincidentally another progress host – his house had been visited by Henry VIII and Anne Boleyn thirty-three years earlier. All of his three daughters and his wife were well provided for, but he had left nothing to the son of his brother in Stowmarket, so, not wishing to be persuaded otherwise, he had kept his intentions very quiet. North, who was not on good terms with Revet, had learned of them in some indirect way

Memorial to Sir Thomas Revet with his two wives and four daughters, including Isbel who died a baby, in St Margaret's Church, Chippenham, Cambridgeshire.

and took the opportunity to do Burghley a favour and himself some good. (Neither scheme came to fruition.)[48]

Thomas Revet died ten days later. He left careful arrangements for the management of his estates while Alice and Anne were under age and detailed instructions for the payment of legacies in cash to his family. His wife and daughters were to receive large sums subject to certain strict conditions, as well as their jewels and rich apparel, and smaller amounts went to his sister and brothers and nieces – though, as Lord North said, not to his nephew. He also left money to a number of godchildren – though he could not remember all their names – and to twenty named servants and others unspecified. Though his two houses must have been richly furnished, the only items he mentioned specifically were two silver-gilt pots bearing the Paget arms, which were to go to his wife. He left no loving messages or personal acknowledgements.

Like Thomas Kytson, Revet remembered his local communities, leaving money to the poor around his London house in the parish of St Margaret's Lothbury and around Chippenham, including 5s each to thirty poor girls when they married; and to two London hospitals, six leper houses and six prisons, including Cambridge Castle, 'for the relief of the poore prisoners'. He also left £200 to the Mercers Company as capital to be used to provide thirteen penny loaves of 'good sweete breade' to be distributed to twelve poor people and the sexton at morning service in St Margaret's and in Chippenham Church. A serious-minded and careful man, conscious of his obligations and duties, Revet also left £20 to the Mercers Company for a dinner to be held at their hall immediately after his death.[49]

Exceptional among the country gentlemen without national pretensions whose houses were used by the Queen, Revet, like Kytson, presented her with a gift. The gold bowl, the lid surmounted by a ring in which were suspended an emerald and three small pearls, reflected his wealth.[50] So no doubt did her entertainment at Chippenham. Churchyard, still with the progress, commented favourably; everything was well organized and the reception generous.

During the Queen's stay letters arrived from the Netherlands and on the Sunday Burghley sent a courier back to Walsingham. The Queen was still being difficult over help for both the Dutch and the Scots and was not pleased with her councillors who advised action. 'We are', said Burghley, 'forced to offend her greatly.' She had, however, signed a formal agreement to borrow some money to be sent to the Netherlands.

Also on the Sunday the Council met with a long agenda. From here on, after nearly two months of travelling, members were becoming less assiduous in their attendance. The Lord Chamberlain, as we have seen, had left ten days earlier. Now Lord Warwick and Sir James Croft absented themselves and each returned for only three more meetings before the progress ended at Greenwich. Perhaps they knew that at Chippenham at least the Council was not to deal with matters of national policy.

Sir Thomas Revet's legacy to the poor of the parish of St Margaret's, Chippenham, as recorded in the church.

What the five remaining councillors considered were several personal pleas for assistance. In response to one, they ordered the London authorities to see that the owners of a merchant ship paid off their sailors fairly. In another case, supported by the Spanish ambassador, they instructed the Bishop of London and certain prison commissioners to look into the complaint of a debtor said to be suffering at the hands of his gaoler. And they wrote to the Lord Justice of Ireland on behalf of a London draper who had acted as guarantor for a Dublin man who had failed to pay up; the draper was now in prison. They also commended the Captain of the Isle of Wight for his pursuit of a pirate and issued orders for the election of the mayor of Dover, now that they had seen the relevant part of the town's charter, which they had called for only six days before at Woodrising.

The following day, Monday 1 September, after two nights and a last dinner at Chippenham, the Queen, the Court and the Council moved on. They turned south again and travelled about 9 miles, skirting Newmarket, to Kirtling, the home of Roger, Lord North. North's father, Edward, the 1st Baron North, was a lawyer who had been a high official under all three previous sovereigns. He owned the former Carthusian priory, the Charterhouse, in London and converted it for use as his home, but in 1530 he had bought the manor of Kirtling and built the house which was to be the family's home for four centuries. On his death, in 1564, Charterhouse was sold, but his son retained rights to certain houses within its precincts.

Roger too became a national figure. Courtier, diplomat and soldier, he was a lifelong friend of Elizabeth and, usually, a supporter of Lord Leicester, with whom he had a family connection; in 1555 he had married the widow of Leicester's eldest brother, who had died aged nineteen at the siege of Boulogne in 1544. His wife, Winifred, was the eighth daughter of Lord Rich, from whose son Leicester had bought the Wanstead house which Elizabeth had visited in May. Sadly, Winifred died soon after the Queen's visit to her house; four years later, her husband planned to marry the Revet heiress.

Roger North was a lively and courageous man. Some years later, aged fifty-five, he accompanied Leicester to the Netherlands to join the English forces fighting for the Dutch and the following year he was shot in the leg the day before the battle of Zutphen (at which Sir Philip Sidney was fatally wounded). Undeterred, he rode into the fray with one boot off and one on. Later still, in 1596, he became Treasurer of the Queen's Household, following Sir Francis Knollys, who held that post from 1570 (and so was with the 1578 progress).[51] North had, as we have seen, accompanied the Queen from Audley End to Norwich and he would have expected to escort her across his county of Cambridgeshire – he was Lord Lieutenant and High Steward of Ely. He continued with the progress when it left Kirtling and returned home only after the Queen had reached Greenwich.

Home was Kirtling Tower, the great moated house built by his father, with its

Kirtling Tower, Cambridgeshire, then called Catledge Hall, as it was in about 1800.

orchards, gardens and courts (only the square brick gatehouse tower survives). Unlike Hengrave and Chippenham, it had been visited by William Bowles and also appeared on the sketch map. Extensive preparations had been made by Usher Anthony Wingfeld, who, coming from Thetford, stayed eight days in all and built both a banqueting house and a 'standing' in the park for the hunting. Although his team's wages were paid by the Queen's Treasurer, it was North who paid for their creations – the 'standing', for example, cost him 25s. He had himself made extensive preparations, building new kitchens and refurbishing other rooms. He had to bring down extra cooks from London and to hire additional pewter dishes.[52] Charles Smythe, Page of Her Majesty's Robes, last occupied at Woodrising a week earlier, now began a particularly busy programme of work, starting with three days at Kirtling, where the final dinner for the French king's ambassador was to be held.

Elizabeth arrived before supper and the lavish entertainments expected in the house of a courtier followed. Churchyard, who saw it all, was full of praise for Lord North's reception of the Queen; he was 'no whit behind any of the best' for his generous hospitality and well-run entertainment. The next day the Queen gave a private dinner for the French party. The comparatively small group of guests – and no

John North's record (in Italian) of the Queen's visit to his home:
  'Saturday 30th The Queen entered our county again, staying in Mr Rivet's house until Sunday
  Sunday 31st September
  Monday 1st Her Majesty came from there after [*sic*] supper to my lord father's house, staying there
  the following Tuesday and Wednesday until the evening, leaving there before supper'
(Bodleian Library MS. Add. C. 193, fol. 40r detail).

doubt also their followers – were served carp and sturgeon, mutton, veal and beef, and fifteen different birds, including not only swans, pheasants, partridges and quail but also godwit, knot, peewit, gulls, dotterel and curlew. The sweet dishes were tarts and fritters with apples, quinces and oranges.[53] The Queen's dishes were brought to the table by local gentlemen and not by her own staff; 'a solemne sighte', said Churchyard, 'for strangers and subiectes to looke uppon'. North's own servants, who would also have been in attendance, wore tawny livery with gold chains and his badge on the left sleeve. Once again a party from Cambridge University arrived, this time to present the Queen with 'a stately and fayre cuppe', accompanied, inevitably, by an oration. All was observed by, and of course designed to impress, 'the Embassadors of France'.

By 8 September the Spanish ambassador in London had heard all about this dinner. He reported to Madrid that after the meal the Queen had talked to the French envoys privately for over an hour. This was in the Presence Chamber (as created for her by the usher and his team), where there would have been a number of other people. The only words that could be overheard by the Spaniard's informant suggested, as indeed might have been guessed, that they were discussing Alençon's intentions. Afterwards Elizabeth had taken Lord Leicester into a corner also for a quiet conversation. Then she asked the French if they would like to play cards, but when they said they would if she wished, she changed tack and said they would do better to take advantage of the presence of the Privy Council – who had of course been present all along – and sent them off for official talks lasting until eight o'clock.[54]

This over, the delegation from the King of France prepared to return home. As a parting gift, de Rambouillet was presented with a basin and ewer, two 'potts' and a pair of flagons, all silver-gilt.[55] They left behind 'Batteville', as Heneage called de Bacqueville, who would not 'give over his sollycitation' on behalf of Alençon. They had been 'most honorably and plentyfully' entertained by Lord North, but the climate at Court was still not to Heneage's liking. The contentious atmosphere persisted and was likely to continue, fostered as it was by certain unnamed persons.[56]

In the midst of all this attention to the French, the Council managed to fit in a short meeting of their own that Tuesday. Sir James Croft, Controller of the Queen's Household – his absence from Court had been noted by Mendoza – reappeared and it was six councillors who dealt with two items, one of rather greater national importance than the other. The first concerned the arrangements for the Queen to borrow money to use in the Netherlands and the following day Burghley wrote again to Walsingham, confirming that she had signed further documents relating to the loans. The Council also considered, probably more briefly, a dispute between a Suffolk parson and a tithe-payer; they decided to refer it to the Bishop and Dean of Norwich.

The Queen departed the following day. Before she left, Lord North presented her with a jewel for which he had paid the large sum of £120. In all, her visit cost him £762 4s 2d, though the Household may have reimbursed him for the Queen's dinner for the French ambassadors. As well as every living creature that could be eaten, including a cartload and two horseloads of oysters, he had provided seventy-four hogsheads of beer, two tuns of ale, six hogsheads of claret and one of white wine, twenty gallons of sack and a hogshead of vinegar. He had spent £89 on 'rewards' to the servants of the Queen and her entourage, £4 on wax candles – no doubt for the Queen's rooms – and torches and 25s on tallow candles. The hired pewter, which had to be cleaned and stored and of which 32s-worth had disappeared, cost in all

£3 10*s* 8*d*. (The losses were replaced later in the year at the great Stourbridge Fair outside Cambridge, the new pewter costing 30*s*.)

North continued to accompany the progress and returned to Kirtling only on 26 September. His quarrel with the Lord Chamberlain which had begun at Melford continued to rankle. Sussex was still complaining about him in November and the Queen herself had to intervene. Nevertheless, he remained in favour until his death at his Charterhouse home in 1600. He was buried at Kirtling, leaving the bulk of his estate to his nineteen-year-old grandson Dudley (whose name marked the North connection with the family of Lord Leicester, his godfather). His father, John, whose pursuit of the progress we have followed, had died three years earlier. Lord North also remembered his younger son and several other grandchildren, and rather belatedly, after all other legacies had been paid, he arranged for something to go to his younger brother, the (now) rather more famous Sir Thomas North, translator of Plutarch's *Lives*, from which Shakespeare drew his classical plots.

He also left money to eight villages around Kirtling and legacies to his servants, twelve, including the cook, by name and the rest listed as 'my gentlemen household servants', 'my yeomen household servants', including two footmen, and 'my menial servants'. Fourteen horses were specifically bequeathed, including a gelding to his secretary and, as an afterthought, 'my black nagge' to Sir John Cuttes, with whom the Queen was to stay later in the progress. Two of his physicians received money and one 'my wroughte velvett cassock . . . and my blacke sattin dublett'.

Three days before he died North added a schedule to his will, primarily to leave £100 in gold to the Queen 'in acknowlegement of my love and duety to Her Majesty from whom I have received advancement to honor and many and continuall favors', praying 'my deere soveraigne' to accept it as a testimony of loyalty.[57]

After dinner at Kirtling on Wednesday 3 September, Elizabeth and her entourage rode the 7 or 8 miles south to Horseheath Hall. Like Kirtling, it had been surveyed by William Bowles and also appeared on the map. The usual preparations were made by Gentleman Usher Symon Bowyer, who came on from Hengrave, and the Wardrobe Yeoman Raphe Hope, who came from Chippenham and stayed for three days.

The Queen's host at Horseheath was the second Sir Giles Alington, a proud but warm-hearted old man. His family had lived at Horseheath since the end of the fourteenth century as important local rather than national figures. This Sir Giles, one of ten children, had succeeded his father, the first Sir Giles, in 1522 and, like his ancestors, had played his part in the county, becoming a magistrate and Sheriff of Cambridgeshire and Huntingdonshire. He had married three times. His first wife, Ursula Drury, great-aunt to Sir William Drury of Hawstead, had died in 1552. So had their eldest son, leaving his father ten grandchildren to bring up. The eldest survivor of these, another Giles, had eventually married and had three children before he also died, in 1573. So his older boy, yet another Giles, became his great-

Roger, Lord North, the Queen's host at Kirtling, aged sixty-five in 1596, when he became Treasurer of the Queen's Household, holding his white wand of office (follower of Marcus Gheeraerts the Younger, private collection, London).

grandfather's heir. Meanwhile, the second Sir Giles had married a widow, Alice Elrington, who in about ten years also gave birth to ten children. In the space of about twenty-five years Horseheath Hall was home to over twenty children. Alice herself died in 1563 and it was Sir Giles's third wife, Margaret, another widow, who was the Queen's hostess. Those of the big families who survived would have left home by 1578, but the three great-grandchildren, boys aged five and six and a girl of seven, would have been there, kept well away from the Court unless invited to appear. It was the six-year-old who was to inherit his great-grandfather's property and wealth when the old man died eight years later and who would eventually become the third Sir Giles.

The Queen's lodging place contained great riches, many of them, as was fashionable, displaying a pride in family history. The house was decorated with forty heraldic shields, ten in the hall, twelve in the parlour and eighteen in the chapel, and Sir Giles lived in considerable style. He drank from his special silver-gilt cup – except when the drink was sack, for which he kept a different gilt cup. Before dinner and after eating oysters he washed his hands in a deep silver bowl and his table was furnished with silver candlesticks, two sets of covered bowls, silver-gilt salts and spoons. His stock of silver included two wine barrels, one with six matching flagons and the other engraved with his initials, a basin and ewer and many other pieces, most of them engraved with the Alington arms. Much of it would have been on display for the Queen's visit and some perhaps added to her own plate for the one dinner she took at Horseheath.

Lady Margaret herself owned rich jewels, including a gold pomander, a great pearl chain, sapphire and turquoise rings, gold chains, an agate decorated with four diamonds and a diamond flower; she could hold her own if invited into the Queen's presence. When Sir Giles died in 1586, his 'deare and welbeloved wife' was to keep the jewels, plate and linen she had brought him when they married and all he had given her since. In addition, she was to have several pieces of silver, her coach and two horses, a wagon with another two and some money. She was, he said, a wife whom he had 'great cause to love, like and trust', for he had seen 'her humble duty, good will and affection towards me and mine'. In fact, when she died six years after him, none of her wealth went to the Alington family. Perhaps because Sir Giles had chosen to be buried with his second wife in Horseheath Church, Margaret was buried with her first husband in London.

Sir Giles left expressions of affection and legacies to all his surviving children and their families and to many friends and servants. Several family members were to have gold rings bearing his arms and Ferdinand Parris, the Norfolk recusant who came from Linton, not far from Horseheath, and who was related to the Alingtons, was to receive a damask gown edged with velvet and furred with marten skins – it must have been very welcome during his spells in prison. Like other local landowners, Sir

Giles remembered the poor of his area and left money to each of four villages, £20 of which was to be distributed on the day of his funeral.

Like his neighbour Lord North, he also had an eye on Lord Burghley's grandchildren and he left a request that his heir should marry a daughter of Sir Thomas Cecil. In this at least he was more favoured than Lord North and the young Giles was indeed married to Dorothy Cecil. He followed the pattern established in three previous generations of this prolific – or well-recorded – family and eventually had at least nine children.[58]

Churchyard, commenting on the progress's entertainment at Horseheath, was not fulsome in his praise but everything went well, he said, and was well liked. Sir Giles had earlier created a very large deer park, where Elizabeth could well have gone hunting while her Council worked.

Her ministers cannot have had much leisure time. On the Thursday they met in Council twice. Only five members attended, Lord Warwick and Sir James Croft again being absent, but once more religion was on the agenda. The only Cambridgeshire recusant on their list, a young local man called Evans Fludd, was examined and found adamant in refusing to attend church. He was sent off to Cambridge, where, like others, he was to be confined and persuaded to conform. The Council instructed a reliable divine, Dr Ithell, to place him in a suitable house, to lecture him and take him to church to hear sermons. He had until Michaelmas to give in. In fact, he took a little longer but at the end of October the Council, hearing that he was 'reclaimed', ordered the Sheriff of Cambridge, with whom he had been lodged, to release him on bail but subject to surveillance. His local ministers were to certify his continuing attendance at church. His conversion evidently did not last, for by the beginning of 1580 he had been imprisoned in Cambridge Castle for over a year and was seriously ill as a result of the cold and narrowness of his cell. He was allowed to move to an approved house, where he could benefit from walks in the garden. This respite was later extended and eventually he recovered. He was released from prison but he never again abandoned his beliefs and continued to be pursued and fined.

The Council also discussed about a dozen other matters of varying importance. To help the Dutch and in response to a request which had come with the support of the Prince of Orange, Her Majesty was 'graciouslie inclined to do them good' and the Council sent instructions to the authorities in London to help Haarlem and Leiden to obtain supplies of English sheepskins over the next four years. They had already discussed at Woodrising and Chippenham their concern about the disputes which regularly arose when the Mayor of Dover was elected. Now the present incumbent was in trouble because he had forced a servant of Sir John Croft on his way through Dover to open his master's mail. The Mayor was to attend their lordships at the end of his term of office. (In fact, he was re-elected.) Other items dealt with that day included the murder of an official courier; three poachers, who were to appear before them at the end of September 'wheresoever the Court shall then be'; the wax figures, which were to be re-examined; and the plague in London, which was beginning to be a serious cause of concern – traders were to be banned from going to the Michaelmas Fair in Canterbury lest they take the infection with them.

The following day, after discussion with the Queen, the Lords of the Council wrote jointly to the English ambassador in Paris. Now that the King of France's envoy was on his way home, Elizabeth wanted Sir Amyas Paulet to know what had been said to him on her behalf by her ministers. When de Rambouillet reported to his master, Paulet would be able to comment on his account of his dealings in England or reinforce the English view. The Council's carefully drafted letter set out five points made by de Rambouillet and the English considered reactions to them.

On the subject of marriage with the Duc d'Alençon, which had the support of the King of France, the Queen had commented rather tartly that she had indeed recently received letters and messengers declaring his love, but since there had been a two-year silence since the proposal was last heard of, she would need to give it some longer consideration.

The second and third points raised by the king's ambassador concerned the official French policy towards Spain and the Netherlands, of which Alençon's activities there might have given a false impression. Elizabeth had been pleased, said the Council, to hear that Henri III also wanted to see the Dutch reconciled to the King of Spain. She too respected Spain's sovereignty in the Netherlands and, the Council added smoothly, the Queen had done all she could by diplomatic means both to protect them from tyranny and to preserve them in their duty to King Philip.

As to the fourth point, France's traditional friendship with Scotland, they need have no anxieties about reports of Scottish approaches to Elizabeth. True, the young King James VI had let her know that, now he was twelve, he was taking over power from his regent Morton and hoped for her continued favour and advice. She was after all his nearest cousin and neighbour and so she had promised him help at any time. Surely in this King Henri would be with her rather than against her.

Finally Henri could rest assured that Mary Queen of Scots was well provided for in England. Any request she made would be met, as long as it had no ulterior motive. The Earl of Shrewsbury, her guardian, had full authority to give her as much freedom as she needed for her health and to replace her staff as necessary, including her old doctor and certain of her servants.

The Council concluded with a request that France should not give asylum to 'rebels, fugitives and bad-disposed persons' from England. The King of Spain had already banished such people from his domains.

The letter was to be carried by Paulet's own servant, Robert Osborne, who had been ready to leave while still at Kirtling two days earlier.

There was further evidence that the progress was approaching its end with the departure of Lord Oxford. He had been with it all along and needed eight carts to carry his belongings back to London. His father-in-law, Lord Burghley, authorizing the expenditure, cannot have been sorry to see him go.

The progress was also slowing down. It is not certain when they left Horseheath but with all the Council business there and their anxiety about the plague ahead, they may well have stayed on until Saturday 6 September. Certainly by 8 September the Spanish ambassador in London had heard that the Queen was delaying her return because of the plague.

CHAPTER 6

THE ROUTE REVISED
6–17 SEPTEMBER

At Horeham Hall

The Queen's next move was towards more familiar territory. Horseheath is close to the Cambridgeshire boundary and as she rode south she was very quickly in Essex, a county she had often visited before. In fact, she had only 3 miles to go to reach Ashdon, where Symon Bowyer and his men had prepared 'a dyninge howse' for her. Some of them must have left Horseheath ahead of the Queen to have all ready for her after the short ride to Ashdon. The rest must have packed up at Horseheath and joined them to finish there after the Queen had gone. In all they spent two days at Ashdon. As usual when the Queen stopped for dinner, a Wardrobe officer was in attendance for the day; on this occasion it was Charles Smythe, coming on from his three days at Kirtling.

Here the owner of the house was a state official. Edward Tyrrell was a member of a large and ancient south Essex family which in the past had produced both eminent and notorious sons, among them, reputedly, the killer of William Rufus, a fifteenth-century Sheriff of Essex and Speaker of the House of Commons and the murderer of the Princes in the Tower. His branch of the family had lived in the Ashdon area since early in the previous century and the house, Waltons, had been built by his grandfather. Edward held two lucrative London appointments. He was Warden of the Fleet Prison, profiting from his right to appoint, in return for a fee, the sub-wardens and gaolers, who in turn exacted payment from the prisoners for every amenity – food and drink, light and bearable accommodation, not to say escape. (No wonder rich men like Thomas Revet left money for poor prisoners!) He was also Keeper of the Palace of Westminster, with the right to let and charge rent for the shops and stalls in Westminster Hall. He would have been considerably more familiar with the ways of the Court than many of the Queen's hosts that summer. Even so he would have had little to do with the dinner.

Some twenty-five years later Edward's son Robert married Susan Millicent, the daughter of Robert Millicent, at whose house in Linton, not far away, the Queen had dined on her way north. Susan was only seventeen, probably a good deal younger than her husband. He was overly fond of the ladies and the marriage broke up. By 1612 Susan and her children had moved out of Waltons, taking with her fifty pieces of silver plate, a jewel set with diamonds and rubies, a 'fair pearl hatband' and much else; she probably included the 'litle jewell of gould called the Shippe enamyled with the unicorns horn placed therein' which her father had left her when he died in 1609.[1]

In the afternoon the Queen, the Court and the Council rode the 7 or 8 miles on to Thaxted, to Horeham Hall, the house of Sir John Cuttes. Horeham had not been on William Bowles's tour of inspection and was not shown on the map of 'the severall howses named in Her Majestie's jestes', both of which expected the Queen to return via Hertfordshire to Hampton Court. The map showed routes from Horseheath to Sawbridgeworth via either 'Cockneth' (Cockenach near Barkway) or Royston. The writer added comments on these houses and was not very flattering about either: Lady Chester's near Barkway was in pleasant surroundings but was a very small house; Mr Chester's at Royston was 'a very unecessary howse for receipt of Her Majestie . . . not haveing any pleasant prospect any way'. The decision to use Horeham instead seems entirely reasonable, but it must have been largely influenced by reports of the plague. Already, before the progress left Kirtling, Heneage had told Walsingham that they were returning through Essex because of the plague in London; the infection could easily be carried up the regular route to the north through Hertfordshire via Hoddesdon, Barkway and Royston.

Such changes of plan were unwelcome not only to the Chamber officers but also to Lord Treasurer Burghley, who was always concerned about the Court's expenditure. Stocks of food and drink and fodder requisitioned by the Purveyors and ready at predetermined points along the route had to be moved or sold off and others organized at short notice and inevitably at extra cost. Nevertheless, Piers Pennante came from Chippenham for his usual six days and Charles Smythe moved straight on from Ashdon to stay four.

John Cuttes was the fifth of a long line of the same name. The first Sir John acquired a property at Childerley in Cambridgeshire towards the end of the fifteenth century and the family lived there for the next hundred years, building themselves a new house in the mid-sixteenth century. The second Sir John rose to become Treasurer of Henry VIII's Household and in 1502 he bought the manor of Horeham, with its old timbered house. In 1514 Catherine of Aragon granted him the manor and borough of adjoining Thaxted. It was he who began the building of the new Horeham Hall, which was not quite finished when he died in 1520. Eventually, as a boy of ten, the fifth Sir John inherited a magnificent show-place of a house, with a great 46 foot hall, longer than the Queen's presence chamber at Havering.[2]

Horeham Hall, Essex, the home of Sir John Cuttes (engraving 1831).

Elizabeth had already stayed there in 1571. On that occasion the progress travelled only as far as Audley End and stopped at Horeham on the way back. A few days later she was at Mark Hall, Latton, the home of John Branch, as we have seen. While the Queen was there, John Cuttes, who, with other Essex gentry, would have been accompanying her across Essex, was knighted by Lord Leicester.

No details of Elizabeth's entertainment on either visit are known. Churchyard did not manage to be there and was not even able to comment on what happened from hearsay. However, John Cuttes was well known for the extravagance of his lifestyle – he was described as 'a most bountifull house-keeper' and was said to have been 'more magnificent than prudent' – so doubtless it was generous. Certainly Elizabeth would have been able to go hunting in Sir John's deer park. Eventually he seems to have felt the effects of his lavish expenditure and by the end of the century he had transferred the manor of Thaxted to the father of his daughter-in-law, Thomas Kemp, and sold Horeham Hall.[3]

In spite of the splendour of Horeham, the Cuttes family regarded Childerley as their home base and the fifth Sir John took no part in Essex politics. Soon after the Queen's visit he married his second wife, Margaret Brockett, of Brockett Hall near Hatfield, which Elizabeth had visited five years before on a short winter trip into

Hertfordshire. She brought him as her dowry more land around Childerley and even before he left Horeham he was active in Cambridgeshire and, with his father-in-law, in Hertfordshire. When he died in 1614, he was buried at Lolworth near Childerley with Margaret, who had died about four years before, and his mother, Sybbella, who had died in London in 1568 and even then had been brought back to be buried there.

On Sunday 7 September the Queen sent for de Bacqueville to give him her reply to his master's proposal of marriage; he had been waiting for it ever since he reached the Court in early August. Only Lord Burghley, Lord Leicester and Sir Christopher Hatton were allowed to hear what was said. Elizabeth first expressed appreciation of Alençon's sending de Bacqueville to her although it had been two years since the question had last been raised and some (though not all) of his excuses were unacceptable. As to the proposal itself, she would say what she had said to 'no small number of princes', that she would not agree to marry anyone she had not first met. Alençon should be well briefed before he decided to come to England. He should be ready to continue their amicable relations even if she did not accept him. If he was not so minded, he should not come. If, however, he wished to visit her, it should be as privately as possible and ostensibly only to see her and her country; then, if his project failed, he need not take offence. Answering a question, she said de Bacqueville could not be shown the papers setting out her terms for the marriage as they were with Walsingham in the Netherlands. However, if Alençon himself asked to see them or at least to be told their content, then Walsingham could go to him.

With this concession, de Bacqueville took his leave and set out to return to his master. Heneage at least must have been glad to see him go. On the following Wednesday four of de Bacqueville's gentlemen who were apparently still at Horeham, preparing to follow their master, received farewell gifts from the Queen. Monsieur de Quissé, who had found favour with Elizabeth and had been entrusted with letters from the Court to the Netherlands early in August, had since returned to England and now on his departure was given a 22 oz gold chain. Two other Frenchmen got lighter chains decorated with seed pearls and enamelled and a third was given a chain of 'gould wyer worke'. Later still two gentlemen of the Court were paid for attending de Bacqueville, with their own followers, while he was in England. One was Edward Stafford, the Gentleman Pensioner whose chain the Queen had given to a Frenchman in Norwich – appropriately enough, for earlier in the year he had been sent to France to assess attitudes there to Alençon's marriage proposal and had formed close contacts with his entourage. The other, Gentleman Usher Richard Brakenbury, was not a regular member of the Chamber but was used from time to time to meet and look after foreign visitors to the Queen; he was paid 6s 8d a day for himself and his men.

The day after de Bacqueville's departure, on the Queen's instructions, Burghley sent Walsingham an account of Sunday's audience, particularly the question of the proposed marriage articles, on which he thought she would not have conceded so much if de

Bacqueville had not pressed her. He had questioned whether they really were with Walsingham but Elizabeth had said briskly that it did not matter, he could tell Alençon what was in them. In fact, Walsingham, replying, said that he neither had the articles nor could remember their substance. Burghley's letter commented that he did not know how the Frenchman had taken Elizabeth's attitude to a visit by Alençon, but 'if I were in his place', he said, 'I should be very loth to provoke my master to come over upon such an uncertain answer'. He concluded gloomily that the realm was likely to suffer either from the Queen's failure to marry or from any husband she might take.

Sir Christopher Hatton also wrote to Walsingham about de Bacqueville's audience with the Queen. He made no attempt to cover the same ground as Burghley but reported that the Frenchman had asked that Walsingham should not leave the Netherlands until Alençon had 'digested' Elizabeth's messages. (A note added to the manuscript suggested that no great weight need be attached to this request.) When he did return, Walsingham would find that his 'wise and discreet proceeding' had been received with 'very good liking' by the Queen and the Council.

As the French party left, John North made his final appearance at the Court on progress. This time he made use of the services of two servants of Lady Howard. This was Catherine, wife of Lord Howard of Effingham and future mother-in-law of Robert Southwell of Woodrising. She was the daughter of Henry Carey, Lord Hunsdon, and granddaughter of Mary Boleyn. Thus she was second cousin to the Queen, to whom she was always close. In 1565 she had carried the baby of Princess Cecilia at his christening in Whitehall Palace (when another young woman, the Swedish Helena, had met her future husband William Parr).[4] Since 1572 she had been Mistress of the Robes and chief Lady of the Privy Chamber and so was travelling with the Queen. She continued at Court until her sudden death in 1603, which came as a heavy blow to the ageing Elizabeth and, it was thought, hastened her own death a month later.

On that same Sunday the Council managed to fit in a short meeting. Seven members attended, Lord Warwick and Sir James Croft having reappeared. Among other items, they considered the condition of the Fens, something of which they may well have seen on their way to and from Chippenham. They instructed the Bishop of Ely and the other Commissioners of Sewears to get on with the clearing out of the drains 'nowe whilest the wether is so drye'.

Another letter went to the Netherlands at this time. The Queen herself wrote indignantly to her ambassadors in reply to a Dutch request for £28,000. The States General evidently did not consider she had done enough for them, although the £20,000 sent in May for mercenary troops had now reached Duke John Casimir. They would get more only if they could agree among themselves that Casimir should have some of it. The ambassadors must make clear to the States that if they persisted in their ingratitude and resistance to Elizabeth's conditions, 'they will force us to withdraw our aid from them, seeing they will no better consider us who have so frankly aided them in their extremity'. However, a more cautious note at the end of the letter authorized discretion in the use of its contents.

On the Tuesday Secretary Wilson wrote both a personal letter to Walsingham and more formally to the two ambassadors. Clearly against his will, he reiterated that no money was to be handed over to the Dutch yet, although he was enclosing the bonds covering the £28,000 they had asked for. The Queen had still not given the word.

All these letters were carried by the Norwich man Nicholas Fante, a servant of Walsingham who had arrived while the Court was at Kenninghall three weeks before and had ridden on with them. Before they left Horseheath the Council had authorized him to hire horses to take him to the coast and shipping to cross to the Netherlands.

Lord Leicester did not immediately contribute to the mail being prepared for the Netherlands. Once de Bacqueville had gone, he felt able to leave the Court and on the Monday he went home to Wanstead. With the change of route, he had urgently to make arrangements for two important events to take place there later in the month. On the Wednesday, however, while there he wrote a short letter to Walsingham, deploring the Queen's reluctance to assist either the States or John Casimir. He set off immediately to ride the 30 or so miles back to Horeham – perhaps he knew he would catch Fante before he left so his letter could go with the rest.

At any rate, he was back at Horeham for the Council meeting the following day. As at Horseheath, the group was reduced to five, with Lord Warwick and Sir James Croft absent again. Now that they had crossed into another county the Council resumed their questioning of suspected recusants. In 1577 the Bishop had supplied forty-six Essex names[5] and fifteen were now chosen to appear before them. One, Rooke Grene of Little Sampford, a gentleman of more modest means than most of the Norfolk recusants summoned by the Council, was interviewed at Horeham, 3 or 4 miles from his home. Like many others, he refused to conform and he was sent off to Saffron Walden to be confined, at his own expense, in the house of the town treasurer; one servant could attend him. Two Protestant preachers were to try to convert him; they could visit him or he had to go to them whenever they wished. The treasurer or some of his servants had to take him to church whenever there was preaching there. If he had not given in by Michaelmas, he was to be imprisoned in the county gaol – as indeed he was. He languished in Colchester Castle until, in June of the following year, the Council agreed to his transfer to a private house to recover his health and, suitably supervised, attend to the affairs of his recently dead father-in-law. Again he was to pay his enforced host for his keep and to provide money guarantees of his remaining there. If he did not conform by 1 November, he was to be returned to prison. He was still listed as a recusant ten years later.

His son, William, and one of his tenants, who, with his wife, had prudently made over their goods to their sons, were also summoned to present themselves. Understandably, they were in no hurry to do so.

While he was at Horeham, Burghley received some news from Dover. No election in the past twenty years had been 'without blowes or scratchinge' but this time the Mayor had been re-elected 'with the greatest quietness'. Evidently the Council's moves to end the controversy there had borne fruit.

About this time another member of the Queen's entourage had permission to leave the Court. Lady Derby went home to Isleworth, her belongings loaded on to three carts – another sign that the progress was nearing its end.

Nevertheless, the pace remained leisurely. They lingered at Horeham for about a week and then ventured briefly into Hertfordshire.

Hertfordshire

The Queen rode south-west from Horeham towards her next lodging at Little Hadham. This was a journey of some 12 to 14 miles so before she left Essex, having ridden 5 or 6 miles, she paused for the midday meal at Manuden Hall, the house of Thomas Crawley. Piers Pennante spent two days on the 'dininge howse' there. He had a particularly busy schedule at this time, having just spent six days at Horeham, coming to Manuden for two and going straight on to Hadham for another six. His team must have split up for at least some of the time. From there, however, they went straight back to Greenwich. Charles Smythe came for the day as usual.

Thomas Crawley's father, a lawyer living at Wenden Lofts, owned a number of manors in north-west Essex and had been sufficiently well off to provide in his will for the establishment of a grammar school for the children of his villages, including Manuden. Earlier one of the Crawley family had been a Protestant and had fled abroad during the reign of Mary Tudor, but Thomas followed the old ways. He and his wife, Margaret, had been named in the previous year's return of recusants – they were the wealthiest on the Essex list. He would have seen nothing of the Queen and her Court while she made use of his house. Indeed, he may already have been under house arrest in Colchester, having been summoned to appear before the Council as soon as they entered Essex. He was examined, probably at Horeham, and was sent to a suitable house in Colchester, to be confined and subject to persuasion until Michaelmas; then, if he still refused to conform, he was to be imprisoned. Whatever the outcome at that time, he was still recorded as a recusant ten years later.[6]

His house was chosen primarily as a suitable and convenient point between the Queen's two lodging places. As we have already seen demonstrated at Lawshall, Euston and East Harling (and also, though less dramatically, at Bracon Ash, Costessey and Woodrising), the Court officials had no scruples about using the houses of recusants. Their surveys of places to be listed on the 'gestes' did not include any details about the owners but it is not credible that Lord Chamberlain Sussex, who was largely responsible for managing the progress and also a member of the Council, did

Hadham Hall, Hertfordshire, the home of Henry Capell, as it was in the early twentieth century.

not know of the anti-Catholic steps to be taken on the way. Such decisions served to demonstrate, in these cases probably intentionally, the supreme power of the Crown.

By the evening of that day, probably Saturday 13 September, the Queen rode through the town of Bishop's Stortford to Hadham Hall, the home of Henry Capell. Usher Piers Pennante came straight on from Manuden and, exceptionally, both Wardrobe officers arrived. Raphe Hope, coming at leisure from Horseheath, stayed four days but the busy Charles Smythe, having been in attendance at Ashdon, Horeham and Manuden, was sent off to London to fetch 'diverse necessaries for Her Majestie' – the progress was not quite at an end yet. He was back three days later.

The Capell family was based at Rayne in Essex, as well as at Little Hadham. At the beginning of the sixteenth century, Sir William Capell, a wealthy draper who was twice Lord Mayor of London, lived near and was buried in St Bartholomew's the Less in the City. He also owned a house at Rayne and he bought the manor of Little Hadham with its old moated house. However, Rayne continued to be the family seat until the 1570s, when the then head of the family, Henry Capell, began building a new house at Hadham. His first wife, Katharine, had died in 1572 and Henry soon moved away to live at Hadham, leaving the Rayne house to be occupied by his son

Arthur when he grew up. Henry's second wife was Mary, widow of Lord John Grey, who had been imprisoned when his brothers Henry, Duke of Suffolk, the father of Lady Jane Grey, and Thomas were executed in 1554 for their part in the Wyatt rebellion against Queen Mary. John's release was facilitated by his wife's family connections. Her brother, Anthony Browne, a staunch Catholic, was favoured by the Queen and he was created 1st Viscount Montague in that year. Dame Mary Grey, like other widows we have seen, retained through her second marriage the superior title she had acquired from her first husband. She had already experienced one royal visit, in 1561, when Elizabeth was staying at Havering and had ridden the mile or so to visit Lord Grey's house at Pyrgo, which she had granted him two years earlier. John Grey died in 1569.

Dame Mary's second husband, Henry Capell, was a local rather than a national figure. He was a Justice of the Peace in Essex and Sheriff of Essex and then Hertfordshire. Besides several manors around Rayne, Hadham and Walkern in Hertfordshire, he owned land in Suffolk, Norfolk and Somerset. When the Queen stayed at his house, he was in his early forties.[7] Like other wealthy gentlemen, Henry was anxious to demonstrate his ancestry and the following year he had his arms painted on the glass of his windows and six heraldic badges made to decorate the house.[8] He was knighted in 1587, only a year before his death. He left legacies to his four sons, the only survivors of his eleven children, and, as agreed with Lord Montague, a generous portion of his lands to his widow. Specifically she was to keep her coach and the two horses 'that doe usually drawe the same'. She was to move to Rayne, where the eldest son, Arthur, had been living and he was to take over Hadham, leaving behind everything listed in the inventory taken when he moved in.[9]

No details survive of the Queen's reception at Hadham, though Churchyard, who was evidently able to observe for himself, found there 'excellente goode cheere and entertaynment'. There was an extensive deer park, so no doubt plenty of hunting took place.

There was also another encounter with Gabriel Harvey, whose appearance at Audley End nearly two months earlier has already been described. Hadham is not much further from Cambridge and his attendance at Court while they were there was probably arranged by his patron, Lord Leicester. This time he was permitted to present the Queen with a copy of a book expanding his Audley End verses, which he had since had printed.[10] In the first poem Harvey described how he was presented to the Queen by Lord Leicester. She allowed him to kiss her hand and commented that he looked like an Italian. Leicester, so near his forthcoming secret marriage, cannot have been pleased to see himself advised in the second poem to marry Elizabeth.

On Sunday 14 September the Privy Council held a meeting at Hadham. Lord Warwick and Sir James Croft were present but Sir Francis Knollys, Treasurer of the Queen's Chamber, was absent for the first time since Kenninghall. It was from

Hadham that the Council sent the Bishop of Norwich his instructions to arrest Lady Jerningham's household priest and to search for any incriminating books and papers. They had evidently received information about his movements that might not have reached the Bishop. They also dealt with reports of a riot in Staffordshire and they issued a letter to a private gentleman 'being beyond the seas for religion' that the Queen had been persuaded to allow him to return home and resume possession of his confiscated property.

Again the plague in London was on their minds. Two recusants imprisoned in the Fleet were to be moved for their safety to reliable Protestant houses 10 or 12 miles out of the city, subject to the usual conditions – that they were to pay for their keep, put down money to ensure that they stayed there and listened to sermons and argument for two months; then, if they had not conformed, they would return to prison. On the day that they took this decision, Lord Burghley received a disturbing report from the bailiff of Hoddesdon, only a dozen or so miles away. A man had died of the plague at the Bell Inn, where travellers regularly lodged; the innkeeper was refusing to obey an order to close his establishment and continued to put up people on their way to the Court.[11]

On this occasion the Council dealt only with home affairs but there was no let-up in the pressure of foreign business. On Monday 15 September the Queen herself wrote to her ambassadors in the Low Countries, replying to a letter from them which had arrived the day before. They had reported moves towards a possible peace agreement between Spain and the States and she instructed them to work for a reduction of forces on all sides. They had also asked permission to return home; they could do so, she said, 'undelayed', if they saw their remaining as not to be for 'our better service' – an admission of defeat which, she implied, would not be welcome.

Secretary Wilson also wrote letters on that Monday. It was he who had received the mail from the Low Countries that had reached the Court the previous day. He had delivered the ambassadors' letter to the Queen and had read to her what they had written to the Council and their enclosures. On her instructions, all had to be sent on to Lord Burghley, who had been allowed to escape briefly to his own house, Theobalds. She had received his reaction and incorporated his views into her letter in time to have it dispatched on the Monday. Wilson enclosed with his own letter to Walsingham and Cobham copies of the mail from the English ambassador in Paris which had also arrived on the Sunday.

All the letters to the ambassadors were carried by a servant of the English agent resident in Antwerp, who had arrived while the Court was at Audley End nearly two months earlier. Wilson enclosed a little note to his master, who had long waited for his return. He apologized for dictating his letter; he would have like to write in his own hand at greater length but he was, he said, 'overwearied with business'. The Council clerks, like their masters, had a busy weekend.

Separately and unofficially, using a private messenger, a friend of Walsingham wrote him an informal, jokey letter from Hadham. He had been hanging about the Court ever since Walsingham's departure, unable to do anything to serve him but pray for his prosperity, success and good health. As to the last, he had worried about the plague in Louvain and the 'Spanish fig' with which the Governor of the Netherlands might have had him poisoned, but he had just had good news from Captain Cockbourne. This was the Scot who had been sent to the Low Countries from Norwich and had arrived at Hadham on the Sunday with the packet of mail which had caused all the letter-writing in reply. Cockbourne had reported that Walsingham was in good health as a result of taking his, Cockbourne's, advice to drink only Rhenish wine, 'which he affirms to be the best physic you can find for your body'.

While he was at Hadham – or perhaps at home at Theobalds – Burghley received some personal mail. A letter from his younger son provided some domestic news. Although when in Norfolk he had been comparatively near his other great house, he had not been allowed to escape there, so Thomas reported on the progress of the building work at Burghley House, near Stamford. The Queen had visited it in 1566 on another long progress, but then much of the building work remained to be done. The new gallery, said Thomas, would be finished by the end of the month, but he advised putting in a ceiling rather than hanging it with tapestries: 'the place is itself subject much to sun and air which will quickly make them fade'. He also commented on the health of his grandmother, always an object of concern for her son. She longed for Burghley to come, for with 'her new sight' – evidently she now had spectacles – she could distinguish faces and 'choose her own meat at the table'. She sent him her blessing.[12]

Another letter, from the Earl of Lincoln, regretted that Burghley had not been given permission for a visit to Burghley House, 'which would have been a good refreshment after the long travel in the Progress'.[13]

The Lord Keeper, Sir Nicholas Bacon, wrote from Norwich, where he was staying with his son Nathaniel (of the velvet coat). Nathaniel was greatly indebted to Burghley, who had been able to do him some service. Earlier, while the progress was at Kirtling, Lord Leicester had written to Bacon senior about his son's standing in the Queen's estimation. The newly knighted Sir Nicholas had been well received at Court, but Elizabeth had listened to someone's disparagement of Nathaniel and had turned against him. Others had had to persuade her that he had been wronged; she was now convinced and spoke favourably of him again. Evidently Burghley had had a hand in this change of heart.

Bacon was concerned that the Queen was 'troubled with the rheum' and also by the advance of the plague. There had been 161 deaths in London the week before last and sixty were infected in St Albans. No wonder the Lord Keeper was in Norfolk![14]

About the same time Sir Christopher Hatton received a letter from Sir Thomas

Jane Cecil, mother of Lord Treasurer Burghley (artist unknown).

Heneage, who had also escaped to his own house, Copthall, in Essex, where the Queen had stayed on her minor progress in May. Both men, as we have seen, were deeply devoted to the Queen and Heneage was able to write freely to Hatton. Like Bacon, he had heard that Elizabeth had been unwell and was anxious to have news of her health, 'which of late hath been more accumbered than she careth for'. Being about to go away for a fortnight or so, he was especially concerned, 'for loving her more than my life, I care for her health more than my own and am in little quiet when I hear that anything impeacheth it'. A few days later Hatton received another letter expressing anxiety about the Queen's health. Reports of her indisposition had reached Lord Sussex in Bath: 'God give her perfect health,' he said, 'for with her good estate we all breathe and live and without that we all stifle and perish.'[15]

Heneage did not mention the plague. Evidently it was not so rife in Essex and it seems to have been thought a safer area, so the progress's next move was back in that direction. The route through Hertfordshire shown on the sketch map had already been abandoned but one house on it (though not on Bowles's list) now provided a convenient stop. With all the business to be done there, the Queen probably stayed at Hadham until Tuesday 16 September. As she rode back through Bishop's Stortford, the church bells were rung, as they always were when she passed; the ringers were paid 10*s* between them for the two occasions.[16] Within a few miles the court and the Council reached Sawbridgeworth and stopped at Hyde Hall.

Symon Bowyer and his men, coming from Horseheath and Ashdon, had plenty of time to prepare the house for her arrival. They would have found it reasonably equipped for their purpose, though Henry Heigham, who lived there – and probably moved out and left it to them – was not the owner. The manor belonged to the Jocelyn family, based in Essex, but Henry, a Suffolk man, had recently married the widow of Richard Jocelyn and moved into her house.[17] Henry was related to the Puritan Heighams of Barrow and to the Jermyns of Rushbrooke, one of whom, Robert, was knighted while the Queen was in Bury St Edmunds. He was in no danger from the Council's scrutiny of their host's religious tendencies.

Henry's wife, Anne, was a member of the Bury St Edmunds Lucas family, so he probably knew her before her marriage to Richard Jocelyn. She brought Henry a stepson and three Jocelyn stepdaughters and she bore him a daughter, Martha, who was still a baby when the Queen stayed in their house.

Henry may not have been a landowner, like some others honoured by the Queen's presence, but he was a wealthy farmer, rearing cattle and making butter and cheese, keeping sheep, pigs and poultry and growing grain. The house was comfortably furnished with chairs as well as forms, stools, featherbeds and silver-gilt tableware.[18]

The Queen probably stayed for only one night. Charles Smythe, on his crowded schedule, came back from his trip to London and spent one day at Hyde Hall. Churchyard did not accompany the progress there and 'hearde of no greate cheere nor banketting'. Nor was any state business recorded there, though about this time Secretary Wilson travelling with the progress and Walsingham in Antwerp would have received letters from Catherine de Medici, Dowager Queen of France and mother of Alençon, seeking support for his proposed marriage with Elizabeth. To Walsingham she expressed her pleasure at reports that Elizabeth was willing to accept him. 'When I see it accomplished,' she said, 'I shall have attained the greatest satisfaction I could receive.' Walsingham, she thought, understood the value such a union would have for the two royal houses and both realms. In fact, he shared Burghley's pessimism about Alençon's suit and had no high expectations of any good resulting from the negotiations, much as he recognized the need for the Queen to marry.

Hyde Hall seems to have simply provided an overnight stop and the next day the progress moved on.

CHAPTER 7

THE END OF SUMMER 17–25 SEPTEMBER

Essex Again

At Hyde Hall Elizabeth was already on the eastern edge of Hertfordshire and now she crossed back into Essex, moving only 6 or 7 miles to Abbess Roding and Rookwood Hall, the house of Wiston Browne. Naturally, it was not on William Bowles's list of houses to be inspected since he had envisaged the return journey further to the west, but Symon Bowyer and his team – or some of them – had come ahead from Sawbridgeworth. By now the ushers' regular pattern of work had broken up, perhaps affected by the change of route or because they were nearly home. There was no more alternating of two or three teams. Anthony Wingfeld's duties had ended at Kirtling and Piers Pennante returned to Greenwich from Hadham. Except for a little help from the part-time Richard Conysbie, Symon Bowyer was left to finish the progress alone. His team must have split up and itself made some kind of leapfrogging arrangements for the next week or so. Their work would be less onerous now that the Queen was to stay only in houses she had visited before and where similar preparations must then have been made. Like Horeham Hall and Mark Hall, Latton, Rookwood Hall had been one of the stops on her return from Audley End in 1571. The Wardrobe men, whose schedule of work was less structured, carried on as usual and Raphe Hope came for three days.

Wiston Browne was a wealthy Essex gentleman. His Abbess Roding land had come down to him from his great-grandfather, Sir Wiston, for whom he was named, and at his father's death twenty years earlier he had inherited the manor of White Roding and other land in the area. Nearly ten years later his great-uncle, judge Sir Anthony Browne, had left his South Weald lands to his stepdaughter, Dorothy. After her death they were to come to Wiston but by the time he died, long before Dorothy, he had already acquired some of them. Wiston Browne thus owned three manor houses: Colvile Hall in White Roding, where he had been born, Weald Hall and Rookwood

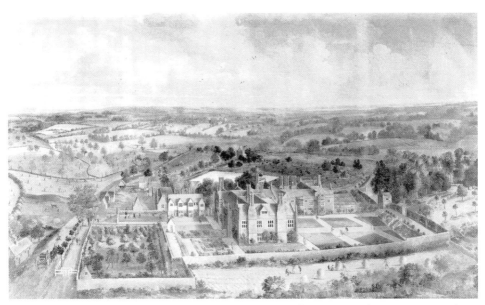

'A Prospect of Weald Hall in the County of Essex' – one of the houses of Wiston Browne, built 1540–50, enlarged 1560–70 (attributed to William van der Hagen).

Hall. All were fully furnished and equipped for comfortable and even elegant living, with silver-gilt tableware, silver plate and books. When he was dying, less than two years after the Queen's second visit, he was anxious that the ceilings and other built-in woodwork, the furnishings of the living quarters, the brewing materials, the kitchen equipment – dresser boards, tubs, troughs, cheese presses and so on – and all the farm outbuildings, bakehouses, dairies and wash-houses, the millstones, the iron fittings and the lead cisterns and gutters should remain in place in each of the houses. Like Robert Millicent of Linton, he wanted to protect his doors, gates and the glass of his windows from plunder after his death.

Wiston Browne had married Mary Capell, the daughter of Henry Capell's brother Edward, and they had had one daughter, Katharine. After Mary died, Wiston married an Essex lady, Elizabeth Paulett, who bore him another daughter, Jane, and a son who was to die in his teens. When they married she gave him a set of gold rings adorned with three rubies and he would give her during their marriage jewels – chains, bracelets and rings – and money to spend as she wished without accounting for it to her husband. Jane eventually married, as her second husband, Gamaliel Capell, third son of Henry, her father's former brother-in-law, who in time acquired Rookwood Hall and began nearly 100 years of Capells there.[1]

At least twice in his life Wiston's rapaciousness provoked the displeasure of the authorities. Quite soon after the death of his great-uncle he appropriated the land donated by Sir Anthony to the grammar school which he had founded. The local inhabitants complained to Lord Keeper Bacon and in 1573 Wiston was ordered to return the school's property. Even so, he managed to put off doing so for another two years.[2] Nevertheless, he was made Sheriff of Essex and Hertfordshire in 1576 and in 1578 he became a Justice of the Peace.

While he was Sheriff, Wiston was again in trouble of his own making. Among Sir Anthony's possessions which he had inherited was St Thomas's Chapel, which the people of Brentwood attended for services, their parish church at South Weald being, they said, too far away. In 1577 Wiston decided to close the chapel, withdrawing the chaplain's stipend and removing the pews which the congregation themselves had installed. On 5 August Thomasine Tyler and thirty or so other women assembled at the chapel, dragged out the schoolmaster and beat him. (His presence is not explained.) Then they barricaded themselves inside and resisted all attempts to dislodge them, using, reported Wiston, 'pitchforks, bills [billhooks], a piked staff, two hot spits, three bows and nine arrows, one hatchet, one great hammer, hot water in two kettles and a great sharp stone'. They gave in only later in the day when Wiston himself and two JPs arrived and arrested about half of them. The others escaped. The women clearly had the support of some of the local men. One, a yeoman, refused to help 'in suppressing the riotous persons' when ordered to do so by one of the JPs and when Thomasine was being taken to prison a labourer attempted to rescue her under the noses of the authorities.[3]

By 7 August the Privy Council had heard about the affair. They summoned Wiston to attend them on 11 August and gave instructions for the fifteen women to be freed on bail immediately. Wiston duly appeared at the Council meeting at Richmond Palace, but the controversy between him and the local population was far from settled. The case against the women and their male supporters was heard at the Michaelmas Quarter Sessions, where the magistrates, as instructed by the Council, imposed only token fines, $4d$ each for the women and $2s$ for the men. The Council's view was that Wiston's own action had been 'the chefest cause' of the riot. The dispute as to Wiston's right to the chapel dragged on into 1578, but eventually, as with the school, he had to give in.

The Queen probably arrived at Rookwood Hall during the afternoon of Wednesday 17 September. Churchyard did not get there – he seems to have left the progress at Hadham – and learned nothing of the entertainment. An attraction for the Queen would have been the extensive deer park that Wiston Browne prized so highly that he made special provision for his keeper and the deer in his will. Edward Humberstone was to retain his job for life, with all its fees and perquisites, and he could keep two cows and two horses in the park. Six loads of 'sweet hay' from certain of Wiston's meadows were to be delivered to him and stored in the new hay-house to feed the deer in the winter and he himself could cut branches for them to browse on. He could continue to live in the room he currently occupied until a new keeper's lodge should be built for him within the park.[4] Perhaps Humberstone's preparations for a royal hunt in his park two years earlier had been satisfactory and were still in his master's mind. No doubt Raphe Hope made sure that there was suitable clothing for the Queen to wear for the sport.

On the Thursday, 18 September, there was a meeting of the Council attended by only five members. For the first time in nearly two months Lord Burghley missed a meeting, probably having briefly escaped again to Theobalds. The brothers Lord Leicester and Lord Warwick were present, however, with Sir Francis Knollys, Sir Christopher Hatton and Secretary Wilson. Once more they were preoccupied with the threatening plague and they issued stringent new orders to limit its spread. The Lord Mayor of London was told to postpone the training of troops due to take place in the city at Michaelmas, all unnecessary gatherings should be delayed and those infected must be isolated from those still in good health. They also now banned all inhabitants of the city from going to the Canterbury Michaelmas Fair. If anyone did get there, he was not to be lodged in the town or allowed to have a stall or even to open his bags to display his wares.

Wiston Browne, already in bad odour with the Council, was also on their list of suspected recusants. Under Edward VI and Mary Tudor, great-uncle Anthony's religious convictions seemed to vary according to those of his sovereign, but when Elizabeth came to the throne he was thought to have retained his Catholic sympathies and was demoted (though he continued as a judge and was knighted some years later). This family association with an accepted Catholic may have been the reason why, later, Wiston was suspected of similar leanings. He had been accused in 1571 of not receiving the sacrament but had claimed that as he was usually in London he took communion there.[5] The Church authorities were evidently not convinced, for he was summoned to appear before the Council when they reached Essex. Where he did so is not recorded – probably he would wisely have obeyed the summons as soon as he received it and not waited till the progress reached Abbess Roding. Wherever it was, the Council felt able to accept his assurance that he had never absented himself from church and his promise that he would continue to attend regularly.

Nevertheless, he must have felt relieved on the Friday when the progress moved on.

That day, 19 September, the progress travelled southwards to Theydon Bois. This was a comparatively short journey of 8 miles or so, but well over half was accomplished before dinner, which was taken at Gaynes Park, Theydon Garnon. Preparations for the meal had been made by Usher Richard Conysbie, who was called on for the first time since Lawshall, his only other assignment during the whole progress. He and seven men spent the usual two days there and Raphe Hope came on from Rookwood Hall for one. Gaynes Park is just east of Copthall, Sir Thomas Heneage's house, which the Queen had visited on her minor progress in May, and close to John Branche's house, where the Queen had dined on her way north two months earlier. Evidently the Court officials recognized the need to spread the load they imposed on the owners of great houses in the areas which the Queen visited most often.

Gaynes Park belonged to Sir William Fitzwilliam, 'comonlie called', as he said, Fitzwilliam 'of Mylton in the countie of Northamptonshire'. Early in the century his grandfather had made his fortune in London as a merchant tailor, eventually becoming an alderman of the city and acquiring lands in Essex. Grandson William, however, still regarded Mylton as the family seat, though he lived there very little. He was a loyal servant of the Crown, spending much of his life in Ireland. Between 1559 and 1573 he was Vice-Treasurer and then Treasurer for the Irish wars and in 1572 he was made Lord Deputy, the Queen's representative there.[6]

When in 1543, aged seventeen, he had married Anne, daughter of Sir William Sidney, Parliament, doubtless at the behest of her father, had decreed that if she should outlive her husband, she should have the use of his Essex lands to live on for the rest of her life. In fact, he survived to return to England in 1575 and would have been at Gaynes Park when the Queen came in 1578. Among her ladies, Anne might have found her sister Frances, wife of Lord Sussex, had she not been taken to Bath for her health, as we saw earlier.

William continued to serve the Queen and in 1587 he was Constable of Fotheringhay Castle, which was in an area of Northamptonshire where he had lands, when Mary Queen of Scots was executed there. On her way to the block she gave him a small gift in recognition of his courtesy towards her.[7] The following year he returned to Ireland as Lord Deputy. One of his first tasks was to deal with the hundreds of survivors of the ships of the Spanish Armada wrecked on the Irish coast, very many of whom were put to death on his orders.[8] He remained in Ireland until he reached the age of seventy and Elizabeth allowed him to retire. He returned to England 'to enioye some fruite of her most godlie and peaceable government', but soon had to endure both blindness and poor health. He remained devoted to Anne, his 'faithfull and comfortable companyon', who had brought up their children largely alone, but seems to have had some doubts about the good faith of their elder son, William, who was to inherit the family lands in Northamptonshire.[9] When he died, in 1599, followed by Anne three years later, his debts to the Queen resulting from his treasurership were still unsettled and they caused a bitter dispute between the sons; John had inherited the Essex lands, but William attempted several times to enter Gaynes Park Hall by force.[10] His father's suspicions seem to have been justified.

Surprisingly, while they were at Gaynes Park the Council held a short meeting to examine the last Essex recusant on their list. Nowhere else on this progress when the

Sir William Fitzwilliam.

Queen halted only to dine was there a meeting of the Council and it looks, in the light of later events, as if this was the last opportunity for three of the members, Leicester, Warwick and Knollys, to attend a meeting to deal with so important a subject as recusancy. In fact, the gentleman who appeared before them, George Scott of Chigwell, agreed to conform to the requirements of the Church and was soon 'dismissed with favour'. The Council members were free to disperse, leaving their clerks to summarize the outcome of all their summonses in Essex. Either the Bishop's list was less reliable than those for the other counties or true recusants were hard to find there. Of the other fourteen men required to present themselves, two, Rooke Grene and Thomas Crawley, were, as we have seen, placed under house arrest. Two others sent back written submissions of conformity and four who came in person claimed that they had always attended church and would continue to do so. These included Wiston Browne and also Henry Bradbury of Littlebury, with whom Lady Derby had lodged while the Court was at Audley End in July. Another, Sir Henry Tyrell, a senior member of the south Essex family, had not appeared because he was ill but his two sons were known to attend church. Three others, including Rooke Grene's son William and one of his tenants, had not yet answered the Council's summons; whether they ever did that year is not recorded, but William and one of the two who had promised in writing to conform were still listed as recusants ten years later.[11]

Later in the day the Queen, the Court and the Council rode another 3 miles or so to Birch Hall, Theydon Bois. This was the home of Dorothy Elrington, whose husband, Edward, had died earlier that year, aged fifty-one. His father had made his fortune as a member of Henry VIII's Household and in 1544 had been granted the office of Chief Butler of England,[12] responsible for the import and supply of wine for the royal table, a post with considerable opportunities for personal profit. Dorothy Elrington was the youngest daughter of Sir Raphe Sadler, at whose Standon house the Queen had stayed in July on her way north. Like Edward Baesh at Stanstead Abbots, Edward Elrington had benefited from his father-in-law's influential position when, for example, he became MP for Wigan in 1572. As well as his lands in Theydon Bois and in north-west Essex around Newport, a few years earlier, again probably with Sir Raphe's help, he had been granted land around High Easter. So he was a wealthy man when he died, leaving five children, four of them still young enough to need special provision for their 'good education and bringing up in learning'. He also left money for rings to be made for his brothers and sisters. Those for the three men were to cost 40s each and to be engraved *Dominus vidit* while the women's were to be 10s cheaper and to say 'The Lord Doth See'.[13]

Dorothy inherited Edward's London house and garden, as well as the Theydon Bois lands and Birch Hall. She already knew what to expect when the Queen arrived, this being Elizabeth's second visit to Birch Hall, where she had stayed in July 1572 at the

The Privy Council's record of the Essex recusant hearings. Rooke Grene and 'Mr Crawley' are the first names on the list (PRO PC2/12 f257).

beginning of a long progress to Warwick and Kenilworth. She would also have known the details of the Queen's visits to her father's house at Standon and her sister's house at Stanstead Abbots.

Preparations for the Queen's stay at her house were made by the now very busy Symon Bowyer and his team, but perhaps because Elizabeth was to leave the next day, no Wardrobe officers came. It must have been a low-key event, for Churchyard heard nothing of it. There were several other substantial houses in the area able to provide good accommodation for the large number of people arriving with the Queen. Some doubtless stayed put when Elizabeth moved on, the distances between stops being now so short.

The next day, Saturday 20 September, the Queen moved to the last of her many lodgings. Luxborough Hall, Chigwell, was no more than 4 miles on; again Elizabeth probably arrived in the afternoon, having dined at Mrs Elrington's before she left. John Stonard, its owner, had already experienced two royal visits, the first in 1561, when Elizabeth rode over from Havering to his other house, Loughton Hall, probably to hunt, and then again in 1576, when she stayed at Luxborough Hall, his new house, at the beginning of another major progress westwards from Essex and then south into Surrey. John Stonard's grandfather had held the lease of the royal manor of Loughton and that Hall seems to have been regarded as the family seat throughout the sixteenth century. When his son George died in 1559, his grandson, another John, inherited his lands but almost immediately he bought the manor of Luxborough and began to build the house which he lived in for the rest of his life.[14] It was much favoured by the Lord Chamberlain – or his officers – and the Queen was to come again on three further occasions (though by then John was dead and his brother Francis was living in the house).

In the 1560s this John Stonard was a High Constable and by the early 1570s he was a Justice of the Peace. Like Wiston Browne, he had to deal with some rioting Essex women. In 1572 another landowner wanted to fence in 61 acres of his woodland. He was entitled to do so with the consent of his tenants, but when they objected he went ahead without it. He then sold the enclosed land, but a large band of men came and broke down the fences. The following spring when the new owner sent his woodsmen in, they were attacked; thirteen women beat them up and seized their axes. A month later an even larger group broke into the woods; the women again assaulted the woodsmen and injured the landowner himself. A week later three JPs, including John Stonard and James Altham from Latton, set up an inquiry into the whole affair (unfortunately the outcome is not known).[15]

John and his wife, Anne, had only one surviving child, Susan, who had married Robert Wroth, another substantial landowner. Their son and heir had been born about two years before the Queen's visit and they probably lived in the old family home, Loughton Hall. Robert had already bought his father-in-law's lease of the manor when John died the following year, aged fifty-seven. Anne was to live in Luxborough Hall for the rest of her life, with half the contents and the use of its farm stock, including twenty-four cows and a bull, six draught oxen and four carthorses to provide for her household. She was also to have five horses of her own. Apart from a few small personal legacies, all John's other possessions, including his plate, jewels and money, went to the already wealthy Robert and Susan.[16] In later years Elizabeth was to visit Robert's house in Enfield.

It was Luxborough Hall that the hard-pressed Symon Bowyer and his men prepared for the Queen's arrival and where Charles Smythe came for two days. Churchyard was not there – though he knew of the Queen's visit – and there is no information on the entertainment at Luxborough. Elizabeth may well have hunted at Loughton, as she did nearly twenty years after, or in Enfield Chase, where Robert Wroth owned land. At all events she was in no hurry to move on.

On Sunday 21 September the Council held its last meeting of the progress. Only Lord Burghley, Sir Christopher Hatton and Secretary Wilson met to instruct the commissioners governing the City of London in their absence about the interrogation of a man arrested there. Lord Leicester, his brother Warwick and Sir Francis Knollys were notably absent. So was Sir James Croft, last recorded at Hadham Hall.

Thereafter, Burghley, who was unwell, was able to leave for Theobalds, only a few miles away, where he stayed to rest and recover for nearly a month. Hatton had an audience with the Queen later in the day, when she was hearing some of the many appeals that were always made to her, and he sent a letter after Burghley reporting her decision on the suit of a friend. She had made a favourable outcome dependent on Burghley's cooperation. Hatton would explain further when they dined together the next day.

That same weekend Lord Burghley, at home, received yet another personal plea for help. During the progress dozens of letters of this kind had reached him. This time a city alderman wrote from London. He was anxious to attend the Lord Treasurer to put his daughter's case against a would-be servant of Burghley, but dared not come for fear of the plague. This was further confirmation of the wisdom of the change of route and when the Queen finally set out first for Greenwich and then Richmond, she would continue to avoid the risk of infection from the city.

A Ceremony and a Celebration

Elizabeth left Luxborough Hall in the morning of Tuesday 23 September. On the way she stopped, as she often had on her long journey, to dine in the house of a subject. But this was no ordinary house; the Queen's last dinner of the progress was at Wanstead, the home of her favourite, Lord Leicester.

He had been at Wanstead since the previous Saturday, when he had had permission to leave the Court, ostensibly no doubt to prepare for the celebration of the end of the progress in three days' time. What Elizabeth did not know, and what no one dared to tell her, was that he was also planning to commit, in her eyes at least, an act of near-betrayal. He was going to be married. His wife, Amy Robsart, had died eighteen years before and there was no legal reason why he should not. But Elizabeth did not like the closest members of her court, men or women, to marry and Leicester was the nearest, most intimate of all. Indeed, many people, among whom Gabriel Harvey was the latest, expected him to marry the Queen. It was for fear of her likely reaction that he had refused to marry Douglas Sheffield, the mother of his only acknowledged son. Now at last, in his mid-forties, he had decided to take the hazardous step.

Some time earlier he had confided to Lord North that, although for years he had avoided marriage for the Queen's sake, he longed to marry 'some godlie gentlewoman' and to have sons to continue his line. North's response was encouraging and Leicester revealed 'the hartie love and affection' that he felt for the Countess of Essex. Lettice, now in her late thirties, was the daughter of Sir Francis Knollys, granddaughter of Mary Boleyn and another second cousin of the Queen. She had married Walter Devereux, 1st Earl of Essex, who had died two years before. (As at the time of Amy's death, there were rumours of murder engineered by Leicester.) Now, as they rode with the progress, North learned that the marriage had been arranged – the bride's father was of course also travelling with them – and when Leicester rode from Luxborough Hall to Wanstead on that Saturday, he took North with him.

That night at supper they found Lord Warwick, Sir Francis Knollys, the Earl of Pembroke, who in his forties had recently married Leicester's teenage niece Mary Sidney, and the bride. After the meal Leicester told North to be up early in the morning, ready for the wedding, and between seven and eight o'clock on the Sunday he and the rest of the party assembled in the little gallery. No wonder attendance at the Council meeting that day was depleted. One of Leicester's chaplains performed the simple ceremony, witnessed by Sir Francis Knollys, who gave his daughter away, the three other supper guests and Lettice's brother Richard.[17] Perhaps because of Douglas Sheffield's experience, Lettice's family were anxious that her union with Leicester should be binding. It was said that they had already gone through some kind of ceremony and that Lettice was pregnant – there is no evidence of either – but this time there was to be no doubt of the legality of the marriage. It was a perforce a quiet occasion.

In contrast, two days later Wanstead was the setting for a truly ostentatious celebration when Leicester gave a magnificent feast for the end of the progress – and Lettice doubtless reappeared in her usual role as one of the ladies of the Court. There was no open mention of the marriage then or for some months. At New Year 'the Countess of Essex' gave the Queen 'a greate cheyne of Amber slightly garnishedd wth golde and small perle',[18] but that was the last time she appeared on the list of givers for over twenty years. Inevitably the story leaked out with time and the following summer it reached Alençon's new representative in England. In August 1579, finding his efforts on behalf of his master opposed by Leicester, he revealed his secret to the Queen. Leicester and Lettice were instantly banished from Court. He was eventually allowed back, suitably humbled, but she was not received again until nearly ten years after Leicester's death when, at the behest of her son, the 2nd Earl of Essex, who had taken his place in the Queen's affections, she was reluctantly allowed into the Queen's presence.[19] For the moment, however, all was well.

As we have seen, Elizabeth had stayed at Wanstead in May at the end of her minor progress. It was not so vast as Leicester's other houses, Leicester House in London and Kenilworth Castle, but she evidently liked it and found it conveniently close to Greenwich. She was to come several more times. It was spacious enough with the fashionable great gallery, the little gallery where the marriage had taken place, and nearly thirty rooms, with all the facilities necessary for a great household – pantries, kitchen, scullery, still-house, brew-house and dairy, as well as the forge and stables. The furnishings were luxurious. The bed in the 'Queen's Chamber' was walnut with a double 'clothe of tinsell' valance, curtains of reversible yellow and purple taffeta and a matching quilt, a down mattress and bolster, a chair and low stool. There was also a square table of inlaid walnut and a cupboard.[20]

Exceptionally, no usher came to prepare a dining house for the Queen – Lord Leicester needed no help in giving a feast for his sovereign – but some of the staff who had accompanied the progress came two days before and were generously accommodated. Perhaps it was their imminent arrival that prompted the early hour of the marriage. Naturally a Wardrobe officer was required to be in attendance; this time it was Charles Smythe, who was already at Luxborough. Churchyard had left the progress at Hadham Hall, but he seems to have returned, perhaps coming back from London and the publisher of his book, which came out later that month. At Wanstead, he said, the progress ended and 'to knit up all, the good chere was revived' with a great celebratory feast for the Queen and the resident French ambassador. Then, in the late afternoon, Elizabeth rode back to the barge which was to take her to Greenwich Palace. Naturally she would have been escorted by her Master of the Horse.

Many people had been busy preparing for her return. A Groom of the Removing Wardrobe of Beddes, who had accompanied the royal furniture on its travels, was sent on ahead from Luxborough to get the Queen's rooms ready, putting up hangings and moving in bedding and other soft furnishings. He, his man and four labourers took four days to set up the royal suite; when she moved on to Richmond, it took them another four days to dismantle everything and brush it clean, ready for storage. Gentleman Usher Piers Pennante and his team had left the progress even earlier; they moved on to Greenwich from Hadham and spent eight days there. As usual a

Lettice Knollys, Countess of Essex, bride of Lord Leicester (George Gower).

Robert Dudley, Earl of Leicester, painted in his mid-forties (artist unknown).

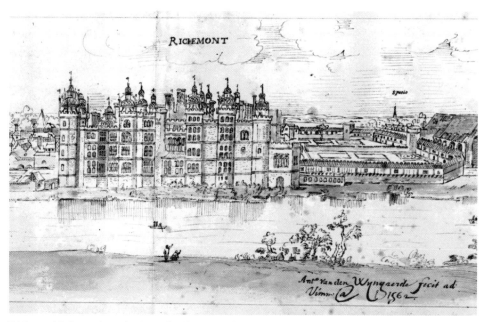

Richmond Palace, where the Court finally settled for the winter (Antony van den Wyngaerde).

Wardrobe officer arrived ahead of the Queen; Raphe Hope came from Gaynes Park to spend three days at Greenwich.

Pennante then went on to arrange somewhere for Elizabeth to rest at Tooting on the way to her palace at Richmond – by a route which would take her well away from the infection of the city. Finally Symon Bowyer took over again, having completed his schedule in Essex since the departure of the other ushers left him on his own at Abbess Roding. Then he went straight from Luxborough to Richmond for another eight days. Rather more time was allowed for preparations at the royal palaces than in the houses of the Queen's subjects.

The Queen stayed at Greenwich only two nights and by Thursday 25 September the Court and Council were settling in at Richmond Palace, where they were to remain until well after Christmas. Everyone must have been glad to be stationary at last after exactly eleven weeks, during which they had stayed in twenty-five different places and dined in ten others. The Queen can only have been pleased with her reception across the most populous part of her realm, particularly the acclaim of her second-largest city. One purpose of the journey, to demonstrate the personality and power of the Queen, had been achieved and many of the valuable gifts presented to her, including six gilt cups and a quantity of gold coin, would go to swell the

Treasury coffers. Certainly the cost of maintaining the Court on progress was higher than when they were settled, but the Council may well have thought the expenditure justified by the success of their other strategy, to give warning by means of the identification and condemnation of a number of locally well-known Catholics that open flouting of the law on religious observance would not be tolerated. But many East Anglian recusants, even if frightened, had not been touched; the worries about affairs abroad remained – there was no peace in the Netherlands – and so did concern for the Queen's health. Her apothecaries' bill for the quarter including the progress was the second highest of the year and by October the pain in her face was as bad as ever; she can have been no easier to deal with. So the summer ended much as it had begun, and the winter routines, culminating in the great festival of Christmas, were once more set in train.

REFERENCES

The Major Sources

For the work of the Gentlemen Ushers and other royal servants and thus the route followed by the progresses: *The Accounts of the Treasurer of the Chamber, Michaelmas 1577–78* (Public Record Office, E351/541 ff. 204–209, 212–213v)

For the work of the Privy Council in domestic and foreign affairs:
The Acts of the Privy Council of England, ed. J.R. Dasent, new series, vol. X: *July 1577–December 1578* (1895)
Calendar of State Papers Domestic Series 1547–1580, ed. R. Lemon (1856) and *Addenda 1566–1579*, ed. M.A. Everett Green (1871)
Calendar of State Papers Foreign Series 1577–78 and *1578–79*, ed. A.J. Butler (1901 and 1903)

For Thomas Churchyard's account of 'The Queenes Majesties Entertaynement in Suffolke and Norfolke' (except in Norwich – see Chapter 4): John Nichols, *The Progresses and Public Processions of Queen Elizabeth* (3 vols, London, 1787 and 1805), vol. III

For the New Year gift lists:
Nichols, *Progresses*, vols II (1787) and III (1805) (except where otherwise indicated)

For some biographical material:
Dictionary of National Biography, ed. L. Steven et al. (63 vols, London, Smith Elder and Co., 1885–1900)

Other sources are given in detail below.

Introduction

1. *Calendar of Spanish State Papers*, ed. Martin A.S. Hume (London, HMSO, 1894), vol. II: *Elizabeth 1568–79*, pp. 50–1

2. Arthur Collins, *Letters and Memorials of State* (2 vols, London, T. Osborne, 1756), p. 210

3. Edmund Lodge, *Illustrations of British History, Biography and Manners* (3 vols, London, 1791), vol. III, p. 135

4. Allegra Woodworth, 'Purveyance for the Royal Household in the Reign of Queen Elizabeth', *Transactions of the American Philosophical Society* new series, XXXV, 1 (1945) p. 28

Chapter 1 Two Progresses: 1 May–11 July

1. Lodge, *Illustrations of British History*, vol. II, p. 170

2. Sir Harris Nicolas, *The Life and Times of Sir Christopher Hatton* (London, Richard Bentley, 1847), p. 51

3. PRO, E351/3213

4. For 6 May and subsequent dates, *The Journal of Sir Francis Walsingham*, ed. C.T. Martin, Camden Miscellany vol. 6 (1871), pp. 36–7.

5. Sir Henry Chauncy, *The Historical Antiquities of Hertfordshire*, reprint (2 vols, Bishop's Stortford, Jim Mullimger, 1826), vol I, p. 380

6. Philip Morant, *The History and Antiquities of Essex* (2 vols, London, 1768), vol. 1, p. 48

7. PRO, PROB 11/86 f253

8. *Sir Philip Sidney, Miscellaneous Prose*, ed. K. Duncan-Jones and J. van Dorsten (Oxford, Clarendon Press, 1973), pp. 21–32

9. Sylvia Freedman, *Poor Penelope* (Bourne End, The Kensal Press, 1983), pp. 48, 153, 165

10. E.M. Tenison, *Elizabethan England Book I 1558–1583* (13 vols, Leamington Spa, 1933), vol. III: *1575–90*, p. 160

11. Historical Manuscripts Commission, *Calendar of the Manuscripts of the Marquess of Salisbury*, part II (London, HMSO, 1888), p. 179

12. Lodge, *Illustrations of British History*, vol. II, p. 171

13. Oxburgh Hall, Norfolk, Bedingfeld Manuscripts

14. PRO, SP 12/125 f46. The standard mile had not yet been established and several versions, all longer than 1,760 yards, were used.

15. *Queen Elizabeth and Her Times, Original Letters*, ed. Thomas Wright (2 vols, London, Henry Colburn, 1838), vol. II, p. 88

Chapter 2 Over Familiar Ground: 11 July–1 August

1. Morant, *History of Essex*, vol. I, p. 19

2. PRO, PROB 11/33 f 9; F.G. Emmison, *Elizabethan Life: Wills of Essex Gentry and Merchants Proved in the Prerogative Court of Canterbury*, Essex Record Office Publications, no. 71 (Chelmsford, Essex County Council, 1978), p. 109

3. PRO, E351/3213

4. *History of the King's Works*, ed. H.M. Colvin (6 vols, HMSO, 1963), vol. II: *The Middle Ages*, p. 958; M.S. Matthews, S.T. Madell and D. Rowland, 'The Structure of Havering Palace', *Essex Journal*, 21, 2 (1986) pp. 28–9; A.C. Edwards, *Elizabethan Essex*, Essex Record Office Publications, no. 34 (Chelmsford, Essex County Council, 1976); Elizabeth E. Ogborne, *History of Essex* (London, 1814), part II, p. 114

5. PRO, SP 12/125 ff40–48

6. Nicolas, *Sir Christopher Hatton*, pp. 68–9

7. Lodge, *Illustrations of British History*, vol. II, p. 187

8. HMC, Salisbury MSS, part II, pp. 189, 190

9. *VCH Essex* (8 vols, Oxford University Press, 1956), vol. IV reprint: *Ongar Hundred*, p. 264

10. Marion Colthorpe and Linley H. Bateman, *Queen Elizabeth and Harlow* (Harlow Development Corporation, 1977) pp. 38–44; F.G. Emmison, *Elizabethan Life: Disorder*, Essex Record Office Publications, no. 56 (Chelmsford, Essex County Council, 1970), p. 322

11. Wright, *Queen Elizabeth and Her Times*, vol. II, p. 87

12. Ibid.

13. HMC, Salisbury MSS, part II, p. 190

14. John Strype, *Annals of the Reformation under Queen Elizabeth* (7 vols, Oxford, Clarendon Press, 1824), vol. II, part II, p. 202

15. H. Cokayne Gibbs, *The Parish Registers of Hunsdon 1546–1837* (London, St Catherine Press, 1915), p. 17

16. Morant, *History of Essex*, vol. II, p. 616

17. PRO, PROB 11/58 f287

18. Neville Williams, *Thomas Howard, Fourth Duke of Norfolk* (London, Barrie and Rockliff, 1964), p. 87

19. PRO, SP 12/81 f111

20. HMC, Salisbury MSS, part II, pp. 188–9

21. Cambridge University Library, University Archives, Letters 9, B13b, B13c

22. Richard, Lord Braybrooke, *The History of Audley End* (London, Samuel Bentley, 1836), p. 77

23. Virginia F. Stern, *Gabriel Harvey* (Oxford, Clarendon Press, 1979), pp. 44–5

24. State Papers Spanish, vol. II, pp. 692, 693; Nicolas, *Sir Christopher Hatton*, p. 150

25. The Bodleian Library Oxford, MS. Add. C. 193 ff38v–39

26. The British Library, Sloane 814 f17

27. Saffron Walden Town Council Archives, Guild of Holy Trinity Accounts; Braybrooke, *Audley End*, pp. 77–8

28. HMC, *Calendar of the MSS of the Marquess of Bath* (London, HMSO, 1980), vol. 5; *Talbot, Dudley and Devereux papers, 1533–1659*, p. 198

Chapter 3 Into the Unknown: 1–16 August

1. PRO, PROB 11/114 f9–10; *VCH Cambs.*, vol. 2 reprint (1967) p. 292
2. William Gurnall, *The Magistrates Pourtraiture* (London, 1656), p. 38
3. College of Arms, Vincent MS 442, *The Commonplace Book of Henry Ferrers, 1549–1633*
4. Ibid
5. Richard Almack, 'Kedington and the Barnardiston Family', *Suffolk Archaeology* IV (1874), p. 123
6. Bodleian, MS. Add. C. 193, f39
7. *Visitations of Suffolk 1561*, ed. J. Jackson Howard (2 vols, London, Golding and Lawrence, 1876), vol. II, p. 40
8. Sir William Parker, *The History of Long Melford* (London, Parker, 1873), p. 329
9. Nichols, *Progresses*, vol. II, p. 21
10. Ibid., vol. III, p. 117
11. *The Register of the Privy Council of Scotland*, ed. D. Masson (16 vols, Edinburgh, 1880), vol III; 1578–1585, p. 23
12. State Papers Spanish, vol II, p. 606
13. Record Office, Bury St Edmunds, Sudbury Town Book 1562–82, f196v
14. Record Office, Bury St Edmunds, Lawshall Parish Register
15. College of Arms, Vincent MS 442
16. *Rushbrooke Parish Registers 1567–1850* (Woodbridge, George Booth, 1903), p. 446
17. College of Arms, Vincent MS 442
18. Diamaid MacCulloch, *Suffolk and the Tudors, Politics and Religion in an English County 1500–1600* (Oxford, Clarendon Press, 1986), p. 201
19. PRO, PROB 11/68 f124v–125v
20. Bodleian, MS. Add. C. 193 f39v
21. Record Office, Bury St Edmunds, St James's Parish Register
22. HMC, Salisbury MSS, Report XIII Add. (London, HMSO, 1915), p. 159
23. Sir John Cullum, *The History and Antiquities of Hawsted*, 2nd edn (London, 1813), p. 156
24. Nichols, *Progresses*, vol. II, p. 54
25. Cullum, *History of Hawsted*, pp. 55, 170, 173
26. C.A. Bradford, *Helena, Marchioness of Northampton* (London, George Allen and Unwin, 1936), p. 69; Nichols, *Progresses*, vol. III, p. 116
27. Record Office, Bury St Edmunds, St James's Parish Register
28. Lodge, *Illustrations of British History*, vol. II, p. 187
29. State Papers Spanish, vol. II, p. 607
30. Bodleian, MS. Add. C. 193 f39v

31. College of Arms, Vincent MS 442

32. Francis Blomefield, *A Topographical History of the County of Norfolk*, 2nd edn (11 vols, London, 1805–10), vol. I, p. 290, vol. VI, pp. 73–4

33. The British Library, Add. MS 27449 ff22–25

34. PRO, SP12/81 ff68–77

35. College of Arms, Vincent MS 442

36. H.W. Saunders, *A History of Norwich Grammar School* (Norwich, Jarrold and Son, 1932), p. 269

37. Norfolk and Norwich Record Office, Pulham St Mary Magdalen, Extracts from the Town Account Book

38. Alison Plowden, *Danger to Elizabeth* (London, Book Club Associates, 1974), p. 113

39. College of Arms, Vincent MS 442

40. Blomefield, *History of Norfolk*, vol. V, p. 24

41. Bartle H.T. Frere, *Amy Robsart of Wymondham* (Norwich, Jarrold and Sons, 1937), p. 20

Chapter 4 Norwich: 16–22 August

The description of Elizabeth's movements and entertainments in Norwich is based (unless otherwise indicated) on:

Bernard Garter's 'The Ioyfull Receyving of the Queenes most excellent Maiestie into hir Highnesse Citie of Norwich' and Thomas Churchyard's 'A Discovrse of the Queenes Maiesties entertainement in Suffolk and Norfolk'; as published in *Records of Early English Drama, Norwich 1540–1642*, ed. D. Galloway (Toronto, University of Toronto Press, 1984), appendix II. The quotations are by the kind permission of UTP.

1. Blomefield, *History of Norfolk*, vol. III, pp. 282, 294; B. Green and R. Young, *Norwich, the Growth of a City* (Hunstanton, Norfolk Museums Service, 1991), p. 24

2. NNRO, Norwich Assembly Minute Book 1568–85, ff162–165

3. *Papers of Nathaniel Bacon*, ed. A. Hassell Smith and Gillian Baker (Norfolk Record Society, 1979), vol. II, p. 19

4. NNRO, Norwich Mayors Court Book 1576–81, f293

5. The British Library, Harleian MS 980 f282; Cambridge University Library microfilm MS6790

6. HMC, 10th Report, vol. II Gaudy MSS, (London, HMSO, 1885), p. 6

7. *Norfolk Archaeology*, vol. I: *Extracts from Original MSS* (1846), pp. 24–5

8. *Early English Drama*, ed. Galloway, pp. xl, xliii, 92

9. H.W. Saunders, 'Gloriana in 1578', 3rd annual report, Friends of Norwich Cathedral (1932), pp. 13–14

10. *Early English Drama*, ed. Galloway, p. 59
11. Saunders, 'Gloriana', p. 15
12. College of Arms, Vincent MS 442
13. Hatfield House Library, CP 161/41–46
14. Wright, *Queen Elizabeth and Her Times*, vol. II, p. 92
15. Blomefield, *History of Norfolk*, vol. II, pp. 411, 415
16. HMC, 10th report, appendix, part IV, MSS of Lord Stafford (London, HMSO, 1885), p. 163
17. Rev. Patrick Ryan, 'Diocesan Returns of Recusants 1577', Miscellanea XII, *Catholic Record Society* XXII (1921), p. 59
18. A. Jessopp, *One Generation of a Norfolk House*, 3rd edn (London, T. Fisher Unwin, 1913), p. 244
19. Lodge, *Illustrations of British History*, vol. II, p. 189
20. John Peter Smith, 'Catholic Registers of Costessey', Miscellanea XII, *CRS* XXII (1921), p. 277
21. Nichols, *Progresses*, vol. II, p. 21
22. C.J. Palmer, *The Perlustration of Great Yarmouth* (Great Yarmouth, George Nall, 1872), vol. I, p. 61; vol. III, p. 252
23. NNRO, Yarmouth Assembly Book, Y/C, 4/272
24. Palmer, *Perlustration*, vol. I, p. 112
25. Nichols, *Progresses*, vol. II, p. 21
26. *Calendar of State Papers Venetian*, ed. Rawdon Brown and G. Cavendish Bentinck (London, HMSO, 1890), vol. VII: *1558–80*, p. 582
27. W.T. Bensley, 'St Leonard's Priory, Norwich', *Norfolk Archaeology* XII (1895), 195–6
28. Saunders, *Norwich Grammar School*, p. 267
29. Nichols, *Progresses*, vol. III, p. 116
30. State Papers Spanish, Vol II, p. 611
31. NNRO, Norwich Assembly Minute Book, f173; *Early English Drama*, ed. Galloway, p. 60
32. King's Lynn Borough Archives, Hall Books 1569–91 no. 5, f156v, 157
33. B. Mackerell, *The History and Antiquities of King's Lynn* (London, 1738), p. 288
34. C.M. Calthrop, *The Palace of Norwich, English Episcopal Palaces*, ed. R.S. Rait (London, Constable and Co., 1910), p. 213
35. Biographical details: A. Hassell Smith, *County and Court, Government and Politics in Norfolk 1558–1603* (Oxford, Clarendon Press, 1974)
36. NNRO, Norwich Mayors Court Book 1576–81, f298
37. College of Arms, W.C. Ceremonies III f89–89v; *Early English Drama*, ed. Galloway, app. I, pp. 241–2
38. Lodge, *Illustrations of British History*, vol. II, p. 187

39. State Papers Spanish, Vol II, pp. 610–11

40. M.J. Armstrong, *History and Antiquities of Norfolk* (Norwich, M. Booth, 1781), vol X, p. 156; Blomefield, *History of Norfolk*, vol. III, p. 354

Chapter 5 Private Lives: 22 August–6 September

1. Ryan, 'Diocesan Returns of Recusants 1577', pp. 54–63

2. M.M.C. Calthrop, 'Recusant Roll No. 1 1592–93', *CRS*, XVIII (1916), pp. 223, 226, 233

3. Strype, *Annals of the Reformation*, vol. II, part II, pp. 343–4

4. Jessopp, *One Generation of a Norfolk House*, p. 225

5. Hassell Smith, *County and Court*, p. 190

6. HMC, Salisbury MSS, part II, p. 208

7. Blomefield, *History of Norfolk*, vol. VII, p. 116

8. HMC, Report V, reprint 1979, The MSS of Pembroke College Cambridge, p. 486

9. Jessopp, *One Generation of a Norfolk House*, p. 175

10. H.A. Wyndham, *The Wyndhams of Norfolk and Somerset* (Oxford University Press, 1939), pp. 123–4

11. Lodge, *Illustrations of British History*, vol. II, p. 189

12. PRO, SP 15/25 f279

13. Strype, *Annals of the Reformation*, vol. III, part I, pp. 248–9

14. Hassell Smith, *County and Court*, p. 225

15. Lodge, *Illustrations of British History*, vol. II, pp. 177–86

16. Hassell Smith, *County and Court*, p. 222

17. L.G. Bolingbroke, 'Two Elizabethan Inventories', *Norfolk Archaeology*, 15 (1904), 94

18. College of Arms, Vincent MS 442

19. Blomefield, *History of Norfolk*, vol. II, p. 506

20. John, Earl of Kimberley, *The Woodhouses of Kimberley* (privately printed, 1887)

21. *The Burrell Collection* (Glasgow Museums and Art Galleries)

22. College of Arms, Vincent MS 442

23. Hassell Smith, *County and Court*, pp. 316, 323

24. Bodleian, MS Add. C. 193 f40

25. NNRO, Transcription of Churchwardens' Account, Shipdham, MS 21562

26. *The Visitation of Norfolk 1563*, ed. G.H. Dashwood (1878), vol. 2, p. 126

27. Jessopp, *One Generation of a Norfolk House*, p. 124

28. Lodge, *Illustrations of British History*, vol. II, p. 104

29. Hassell Smith, *County and Court*, p. 324

30. 'Recusant Documents from the Ellesmere MSS', ed. A.G. Petti, *CRS*, 60 (1968), p. 107

31. Jessopp, *One Generation of a Norfolk House*, p. 239
32. Thomas Martin, *The History of Thetford* (London, J. Nicholls, 1779), pp. 220–1.
33. Thetford Town Archives, Thetford Assembly Book, T/C1/1 ff9–14v
34. Ibid., T/C1/11 f234
35. PRO, SP 12/81 f81v
36. The British Library, Add. MS 27449 f75
37. Longleat, Thynne Papers, vol. LII, f82
38. Thetford Assembly Book, T/C1/1 f15v
39. John Gage, *The History and Antiquities of Hengrave* (London, James Carpenter, 1822), pp. 21–37, 124, 178, 186–9
40. *Visitation of Suffolk 1561*, part I, p. 59
41. Gage, *History of Hengrave*, p. 23 note
42. Ryan, 'Diocesan Returns of Recusants 1577', pp. 6–7
43. MacCulloch, *Suffolk and the Tudors*, p. 195 note
44. HMC, 10th Report, vol. II, Gawdy MSS (London, 1885) p. 11
45. PRO, SP 15/25 f113
46. A.G.H. Hollingsworth, *The History of Stowmarket* (Ipswich, F. Pawsey, 1844), p. 131
47. Memorial, St Margaret's Church, Chippenham; Cambridge Record Office, Parish Registers, Chippenham; The British Library, Harleian MS 5177 f277
48. HMC, Salisbury MSS, part II, p. 523
49. PRO, PROB 11/65 ff91–93
50. Nichols, *Progresses*, vol. II, p. 21
51. Lady Frances Bushby, *Three Men of the Tudor Time* (London, David Nutt, 1911), pp. 121, 148
52. W. Stevenson, 'The Household Book of Lord North, item xxxii', *Archaeologia* XIX (1821), pp. 290, 298
53. The British Library, Royal Household Book, Add. 34320 f103v
54. State Papers Spanish, vol. II, p. 612
55. Nichols, *Progresses*, vol. III, p. 116
56. PRO, SP15/25 f114
57. PRO, PROB 11/97 ff43–45v
58. Catherine E. Parsons, 'Horseheath Hall and Its Owners', *Cambridge Antiquarian Society Proceedings*, XLI (1948), pp. 7–9; PRO, PROB 11/69 ff376–377v

Chapter 6 The Route Revised: 6–17 September

1. Robert Gibson, *Annals of Ashdon* (Chelmsford, Essex Record Office, 1988), pp. 74–5
2. Christopher Parish, 'The Cuttes Family and Cambridgeshire', *Family History*

Journal, I (1977–8), book 6, 87–90; J.C. Paget, *Horeham Hall* (Essex Record Office papers ERO T/1 box)

3. Morant, *History of Essex*, vol. II, p. 439; Thomas Fuller, *The Worthies of England*, ed. J. Nichols (London, 1811), vol. I, p. 177

4. See Chapter 3, To Bury St Edmunds

5. Ryan, 'Diocesan Returns of Recusants 1577', p. 7

6. Ibid., p. 122; PRO, PROB 11/2 f47; F.G. Emmison, *Essex Gentry's Wills*, pp. 73–4; F.G. Emmison, *Elizabethan Life: Morals and the Church Courts* (Chelmsford, Essex County Council, 1973), Essex Record Office Publications, no. 63, p. 304

7. W. Minet, *Hadham Hall* (privately printed, 1914), pp. viii, 10; Chauncy, *Hertfordshire*, pp. 307–8; W. Addison, *Essex Worthies* (Chichester, Phillimore and Co., 1973), p. 53; *VCH Essex*, vol. IV, p. 52

8. The British Library, Capell Account, Add. MS 63650A

9. PRO, PROB 11/72 f380–380v

10. Edmund Spenser, *The Shepheardes Calender*, 1579, ed. E. de Selincourt (Oxford University Press, 1940), gloss on 'Eclogue 9 September', 1579, p. 455

11. PRO, SP 12/125 f64

12. HMC, Salisbury MSS, part II, p. 200

13. Ibid., p. 201

14. Ibid.

15. Nicolas, *Sir Christopher Hatton*, p. 91

16. Hertfordshire Record Office, Bishop's Stortford Parish Register transcript

17. P. Clutterbuck, *History and Antiquities of Hertfordshire* (3 vols, London, 1827), vol. III, p. 204

18. PRO, PROB 11/72 f168–169

Chapter 7 The End of Summer: 17–25 September

1. *VCH Essex*, vol. VIII, pp. 80, 100–101; vol. IV, p. 192; Morant, *History of Essex*, vol. I, p. 138; PRO, PROB 11/24 f15; Emmison, *Essex Gentry's Wills*, pp. 60–4

2. Gladys Ward, *A History of South Weald and Brentwood* (Waddon, Spenser Press, 1961), p. 21

3. Emmison, *Elizabethan Life: Disorder*, pp. 106–7

4. PRO, PROB 11/24 f15

5. Morant, *History of Essex*, vol. I, p. 118; Emmison, *Elizabethan Life: Morals and the Church Courts*, p. 102

6. Morant, *History of Essex*, vol. I, p. 160

7. Antonia Fraser, *Mary Queen of Scots*, reprint (London, Panther Books Ltd, 1972), p. 630

8. Jasper Ridley, *Elizabeth I* (London, Constable, 1987), p. 289

9. PRO, PROB 11/94 ff127v–129v. He was buried in Marholm Church, close to Milton Hall (near Peterborough)

10. Emmison, *Elizabethan Life: Disorder*, p. 123

11. J.H. Pollen, 'Recusants and Priests, March 1588', Miscellanea XII, *CRS*, XXII (19), p. 122

12. *Letters and Papers of the Reign of Henry VIII*, vol. XIX, part I (London, HMSO 1903, reprint 1965), p. 501

13. PRO, PROB 11/22 f11; Emmison, *Essex Gentry's Wills*, pp. 80–1

14. *VCH Essex*, vol. IV, p. 118; *Essex Archaeological Society*, new series, 8, pp. 146–8

15. Emmison, *Elizabethan Life: Disorder*, pp. 101–2

16. PRO, PROB 11/23 f50; Emmison, *Essex Gentry's Wills*, pp. 129–30

17. *Collins Peerage of England* (9 vols, London, 1812), vol. 4, pp. 461–2; E.M. Tennison, *Elizabethan England*, vol. III: *1575–80*. pp. 161–2

18. The British Library, Sloane 817 f16

19. *Letters and Memorials of State (Sidney Papers)*, ed. A. Collins (2 vols, London, 1746), vol. II, p. 93

20. The British Library, Inventory post-mortem, Harleian Roll D35 ff24–37

FURTHER READING

Addison, Sir William. *The Old Roads of England*, Batsford, 1980

Black, J.B. *The Reign of Elizabeth 1558–1603*, Oxford University Press, 1959

Burton, Elizabeth. *The Elizabethans at Home*, Secker and Warburg Ltd, 1958

Byrne, Muriel St Claire. *Elizabethan Life in Town and Country*, reprint Alan Sutton Publishing, 1987

Chambers, E.K. *The Elizabethan Stage*, vols I–IV, Oxford University Press, 1951

Dodd, A.H. *Elizabethan England*, Batsford and Book Club Associates 1974

Dunlop, Ian. *Palaces and Progresses of Elizabeth I*, Jonathan Cape, 1962

Haigh, Christopher. *Elizabeth I*, Longman, 1988

Jenkins, Elizabeth. *Elizabeth the Great*, Victor Gollancz, 1958

——. *Elizabeth and Leicester*, Victor Gollancz, 1961

Loades, David. *The Tudor Court*, Batsford, 1986

Neale, J.E. *Queen Elizabeth I*, Jonathan Cape, 1934

Plowden, Alison. *The Young Elizabeth*, Macmillan, 1971

——. *Elizabethan England*, Reader's Digest, 1982

Pound, John. *Tudor and Stuart Norwich*, Phillimore and Co., 1988

Read, Conyers. *Lord Burghley and Queen Elizabeth*, Jonathan Cape, 1960

Rowse, A.L., *The England of Elizabeth*, Macmillan, 1950

Somerset, Anne. *Elizabeth I*, Weidenfeld & Nicolson, 1991

Starkey, David (ed.). *Rivals in Power*, Macmillan 1990

Strickland, Agnes. *The Life of Queen Elizabeth*, J.M. Dent, 1906

Thorne, James. *Handbook to the Environs of London*, Godfrey Cave Associates Ltd, 1983

Thurley, Simon. *The Royal Palaces of Tudor England*, Yale University Press, 1993

Wedgwood, C.V. *William the Silent*, Jonathan Cape, 1944

Weinstein, Rosemary. *Tudor London*, HMSO, 1994

Williams, Neville. *Thomas Howard, Fourth Duke of Norfolk*, Barrie Books Ltd, 1964

——. *Elizabeth I Queen of England*, Weidenfeld & Nicolson, 1967

——. *The Life and Times of Elizabeth I*, Weidenfeld & Nicolson and Book Club Associates, 1972

INDEX